IMPRESSIONS of home™
HOMES DESIGNED FOR THE WAY YOU LIVE

MW00573336

EDITOR	Bruce Arant
PLANS EDITOR	Tina Leyden
GRAPHIC DESIGNERS	Yen Gutowski
	Jeff Dedlow
	Heather Guthrie
	Mary Fitzmaurice
ILLUSTRATOR	Heather Guthrie
RENDERING COLORIZATION	Alva Louden
RENDERING ILLUSTRATORS	Shawn Doherty
	Silvia Boyd
	Perry Gauthier
	George McDonald, dec.
TECHNICAL ADVISER	Rob Phillips
PUBLICATIONS ASSISTANT	Lori Walling
CIRCULATION MANAGER	Priscilla Ivey
PUBLISHER	Dennis Brozak
ASSOCIATE PUBLISHER	Linda Reimer

IMPRESSIONS of home™
HOMES DESIGNED FOR THE WAY YOU LIVE

IS PUBLISHED BY:
Design Basics Publications
11112 John Galt Blvd., Omaha, NE 68137
Web – www.designbasics.com
E-Mail – info@designbasics.com

CHIEF EXECUTIVE OFFICER	Dennis Brozak
PRESIDENT	Linda Reimer
DIRECTOR OF MARKETING	Kevin Blair
BUSINESS DEVELOPMENT	Paul Foresman
CONTROLLER	Janie Murnane
EDITOR IN CHIEF	Bruce Arant

COVER PHOTO: Plan #48B-1863 Andover
As seen on page 68

BUILDER: Feledy Construction, Inc.

HOME PLAN DESIGN SERVICE

LIBRARY OF CONGRESS NUMBER: 99-074588
ISBN: 1-892150-15-8

ONE-STORY HOME PLANS

1 1/2-STORY HOME PLANS

1 1/2-STORY HOME PLANS

TWO-STORY HOME PLANS

the Way You Live

With regard to homes, nothing is more personal than what's behind the front door. Than where the kitchen is. Than where the medicine cabinet is in the bathroom. While the exterior of a home is what most will see, the interior is only for a privileged few on occasion. What's inside is for you and your family every day.

But if you're like most until you began your search for a home plan, you may have never really given the interior room arrangement of your home much thought or attention. Whether you realize it or not, defining what you need or simply desire inside your home, is a process of self-discovery. It's thinking about who you are, who your family is and how you live from day to day. It is the reason they say homes reveal us as persons.

It means defining not only the way you live now, but also the way you want to live in the future. It's why you'll desire to have your kitchen to the front - because you want to see those entering your driveway. Or it's why you'll want it to the rear, to watch the sun set as you finish the dishes. It's deciding where you'll want the stairway to be and how many closets should be placed in the halls. It's how close the laundry room will or will not be to the bedrooms and where the refrigerator will be in proximity to the sink and stove.

IMPRESSIONS *of home*™ - *Homes Designed For The Way You Live,* can help you define the interior of your home through your own process of discovery. Specific areas of the home are highlighted among three design perspectives offering varying ideas and design solutions. A deeper perspective of each floor plan is provided from either the designers who created the floor plans, or the homeowners who've lived in them. Also included is a worksheet on pages 82-83 to help you organize your ideas on paper. Turn the page and let IMPRESSIONS *of home*™ help you begin this rewarding "interior" journey of discovery.

A. *Briarton*

#48B-5503   *Price Code A25*

2586 Finished Sq. Ft.

NOTE: 9 ft. main level walls

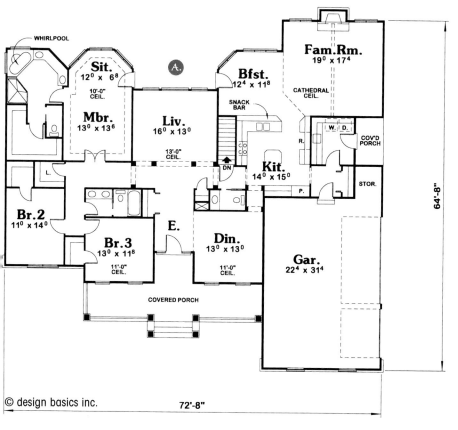

THINK ABOUT...
EXTERIOR VIEWS

Exterior views are not only important for enjoying the visual appeal of your lot, but they're also important for bringing light into rooms within your home. Exterior views can enhance a room, such as a dining room, where your guests can enjoy a view to the front while they dine. Consider the views within each room of your home and how they compare to the views your lot will offer. A view of the golf course from your living room will be enjoyed for many years, whereas a view of the side of your neighbor's house may only provide regret.

3 PERSPECTIVES...

A. The dominant views in the Briarton take advantage of a lot with a rear view. The family room, breakfast area, living room and master suite sitting room, all enjoy plenty of natural light.

B. The most stunning view in the Ashley Acres is located within the family room. A cathedral ceiling tops a tall group of four windows with trapezoid-shaped transoms.

C. While the two-story living room creates a dominating view in the Troon Manor, other views are provided throughout the home. Especially striking, the second-story balcony has a dramatic view to the back through the second-story windows of the living room. The master suite, study loft and bedroom 2 also take advantage of views to the back.

B. Ashley Acres

#48B-8056   *Price Code* A23

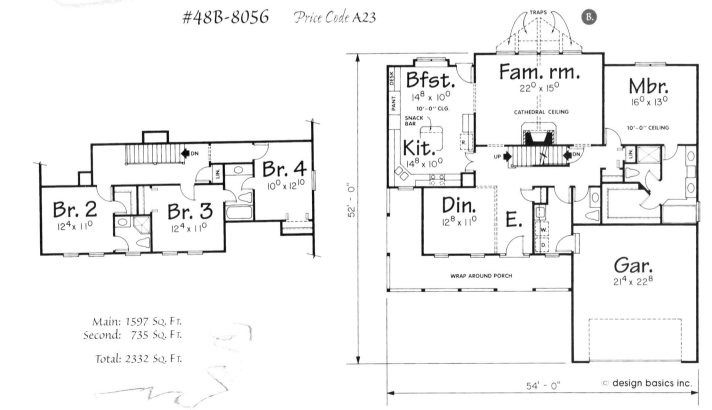

Room	Dimensions
Bfst.	14⁸ x 10⁰

Bfst. 14⁸ x 10⁰ — 10'-0" CLG.

SNACK BAR

Kit. 14⁸ x 10⁰

Fam. rm. 22⁰ x 15⁰ — CATHEDRAL CEILING

Mbr. 16⁰ x 13⁰ — 10'-0" CEILING

UP   DN

Din. 12⁸ x 11⁰

E.

W. D.

Gar. 21⁴ x 22⁸

WRAP AROUND PORCH

TRAPS

52' - 0"

54' - 0"

© design basics inc.

Br. 2 12⁴ x 11⁰

Br. 3 12⁴ x 11⁰

Br. 4 10⁰ x 12¹⁰

DN

LIN.

Main: 1597 Sq. Ft.
Second: 735 Sq. Ft.

Total: 2332 Sq. Ft.

IMPRESSIONS– Homes designed for the way you live

C. Troon Manor

#48B-9166   *Price Code* B23

Main: 1649 Sq. Ft.
Second: 712 Sq. Ft.

Total: 2361 Sq. Ft.

Slab and Basement Foundation Plans Included.

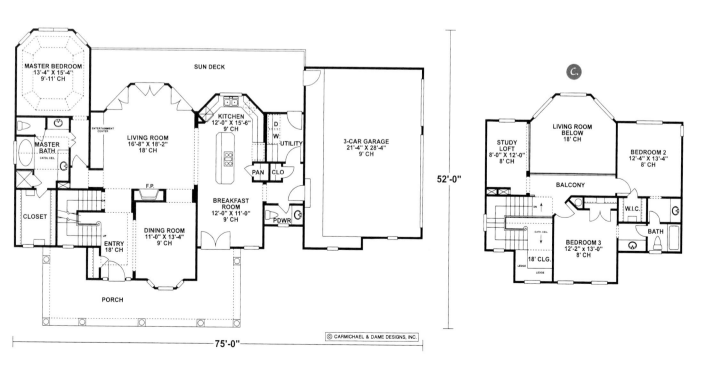

© CARMICHAEL & DAME DESIGNS, INC.

design basics inc.
HOME PLAN DESIGN SERVICE

HOME OWNER IMPRESSIONS

ON LIVING IN THE HALLBROOK

It just might be the million-dollar question: What type of home would a home builder elect to build for himself? For home builder Dave Bilstad, his wife Mary and their two daughters, it's been many homes through the years. In fact, at one point in time, the couple moved six times in six years. But for the last four years, their home has been Design Basics' "Hallbrook."

"We've lived in several Design Basics' homes over the years," Mary says, "But this one is the one we're most comfortable in. It seems to have all the best aspects of every other Design Basics' home we've lived in all rolled into one."

The spaciousness of the Hallbrook offered them an opportunity to create private areas for each member of the household. The Hallbrook's master suite includes a sitting area and access to a deck that created a haven for Dave and Mary. One of the bedrooms on the upper level was utilized as a study area for one daughter who also used an upstairs bedroom and bath. In the lower level basement, they created a large

bedroom, sitting area and bath for their second daughter. "This home allowed each of us to have our own floor," Mary says.

There were two main areas of the Hallbrook that captured the attention of Dave and Mary: the home's main-floor master suite and the elevated den. The other

continued on page 8

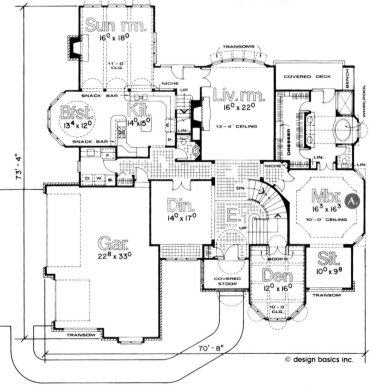

IMPRESSIONS– *Homes designed for the way you live*

A. Hallbrook

#48B-2655   *Price Code* A37

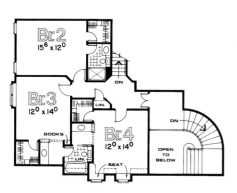

Br. 2
15⁶ x 12⁰

Br. 3
12⁰ x 14⁰

BOOKS

LIN.

DN

DN

Br. 4
12⁰ x 14⁰

LIN.

SEAT

OPEN
TO
BELOW

Main: 2804 Sq. Ft.
Second: 961 Sq. Ft.

Total: 3765 Sq. Ft.

THINK ABOUT...
MASTER SUITE AMENITIES

As you look for the floor plan that best meets all your needs and desires why not splurge a little and give yourself the true retreat you've always desired. The best place to do this is, without a doubt, in the master suite. Maybe you've always wanted a whirlpool tub, a sitting room or a porch - a place to get away from the noise of the television or your childrens music. Perhaps your budget would even allow a built-in entertainment center or a fireplace. And certainly, if you must rationalize such a purchase - tell others you only mean to enhance your home's resale value.

3 PERSPECTIVES...

A. Besides a private sitting room, the Hallbrook's master suite showcases a generous bath. A sloped ceiling visually ties a whirlpool tub and dual-sink vanity together. A large walk-in closet includes a built-in dresser and allows one to get ready without disturbing a sleeping spouse.

B. You can't get much more of a retreat than the master suite in the Clayton. It features a fireplace, sitting room, private porch, whirlpool tub and spacious walk-in closet with his and her compartments.

C. A built-in entertainment center allows those in the master suite of the Norwood to enjoy a favorite program while retiring for the evening or getting ready for the day. A corner whirlpool and large shower are also luxuries that will be appreciated.

homes we've lived in were two-story homes. With our children getting older, we sort of progressed to this plan," Dave says. Dave and Mary utilize the den as a library with floor-to-ceiling bookshelves and a rolling ladder. "It has three beautiful windows which make it kind of a cozy getaway spot in this home," Mary says.

The open area between the kitchen, breakfast area and sunroom is also a place where the Bilstads spend a lot of their time. Most evenings you'll find them cooking the evening meal in the kitchen or, in wintertime, enjoying the warmth of the fireplace in the sunroom, Dave says.

But besides the practical features of the home, the undeniable charm of the Hallbrook captured their emotions. Mary, who owns an interior decorating business, remembers the visual elements within the home when first looking at the floor plan. "There were just so many spaces in this home to create really fun areas - the arches off the kitchen, the elevated library and the huge basement. I remember being attracted to all those things about this home," Mary says.

As owner of his own construction firm, Dave works out of a home office, also located in the basement. The home also serves as a showpiece for clients who want to see the type of craftsmanship he puts into his homes. The home will also serve as this year's Christmas House in their area with all the money raised going to charity.

In retrospect, one might say the home a home builder elects to build for himself is not all that different than one built for someone with no ties to the industry. It is simply a home that meets his family's needs.

B. Clayton

#48B- 5510   *Price Code* A34

Main: 2454 SQ. FT.
Second: 986 SQ. FT.

Total: 3440 SQ. FT.

NOTE: 9 ft. main level walls

Br.2 15³ x 12⁰

OPEN TO BELOW

PLANT SHELF

DESK

Br.4 13⁰ x 11¹⁰

Br.3 12⁰ x 14²

10'-0" CEIL.

OPEN TO BELOW

Sit. 10⁰ x 6⁰

COVERED PORCH

ENT. CENTER

Mbr. 18³ x 15⁰

11'-0" CEIL.

WHIRLPOOL

Grt.Rm 16³ x 21⁰

18'-2" CEIL.

BOOKS

Hrth. 15³ x 16⁸

Bfst. 10⁸ x 12⁸

SNACK BAR

Kit. 12⁸ x 11³

E.

Din. 13³ x 14⁶

BOOKS

Den 12⁰ x 14⁴

10'-0" CEIL.

COVERED PORCH

Gar. 20⁸ x 31⁰

59'-4"

73'-4"

© design basics inc.

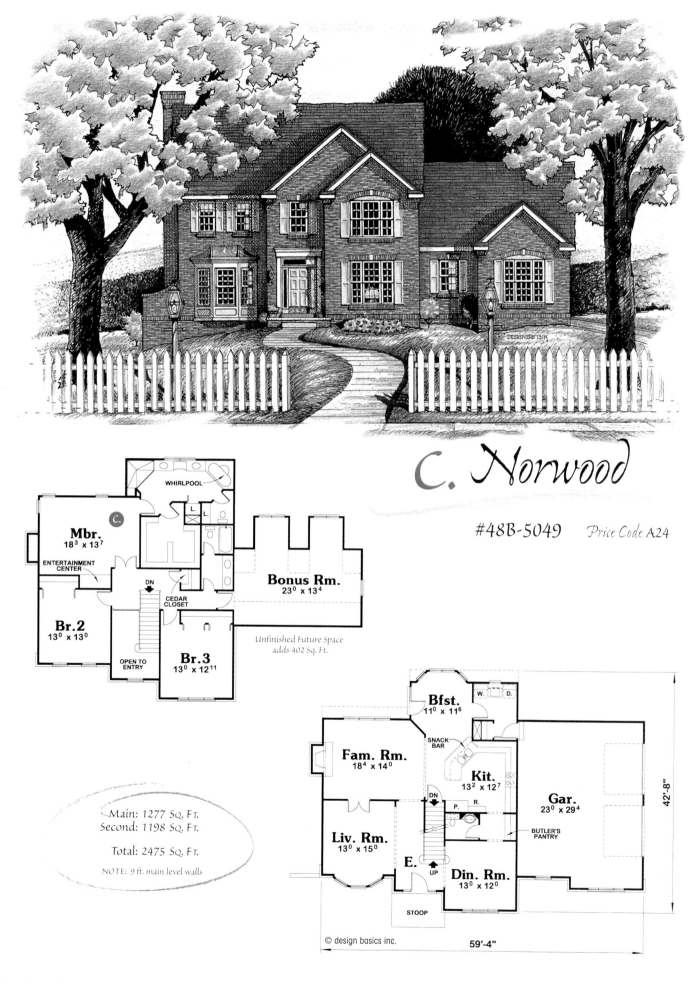

C. Norwood

#48B-5049   *Price Code A24*

WHIRLPOOL

Mbr.
18³ x 13⁷

ENTERTAINMENT CENTER

L. **L.**

DN

CEDAR CLOSET

Bonus Rm.
23⁰ x 13⁴

Br.2
13⁰ x 13⁰

Br.3
13⁰ x 12¹¹

OPEN TO ENTRY

Unfinished Future Space adds 402 Sq. Ft.

Main: 1277 Sq. Ft.
Second: 1198 Sq. Ft.

Total: 2475 Sq. Ft.

NOTE: 9 ft. main level walls

Bfst.
11⁰ x 11⁶

W. **D.**

SNACK BAR

Fam. Rm.
18⁴ x 14⁰

Kit.
13² x 12⁷

Gar.
23⁰ x 29⁴

DN

P. **R.**

BUTLER'S PANTRY

Liv. Rm.
13⁰ x 15⁰

E.

UP

Din. Rm.
13⁰ x 12⁰

STOOP

© design basics inc.

59'-4"

42'-8"

#48B-2649   *Price Code* A 26

Lancaster

#48B-1752   *Price Code* A 18

All areas will be filled with light through
windows that line the rear of the home.

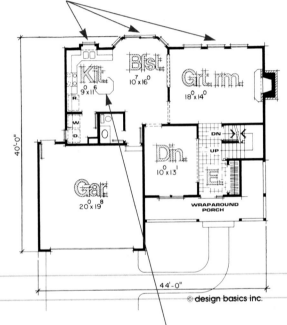

© design basics inc.

French doors offer beauty to both the master bath and bedroom.

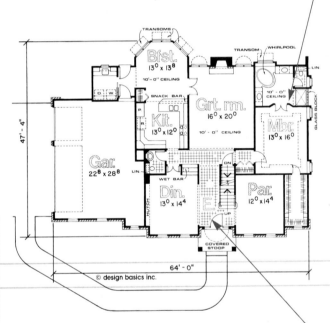

© design basics inc.

Main: 919 Sq. Ft.
Second: 927 Sq. Ft.

Total: 1846 Sq. Ft.

Slab and Basement Foundation Plans Included.

The kitchen's open design allows
it to access many areas efficiently.

The views in this entry are incredible: formal rooms to
either side and an upper-level balcony with built-in seat.

The master suite will be appreciated for its
tiered ceiling and walk-in closets for two.

Two of three second-level bedrooms
feature walk-in closets.

Main: 1865 Sq. Ft.
Second: 774 Sq. Ft.

Total: 2639 Sq. Ft.

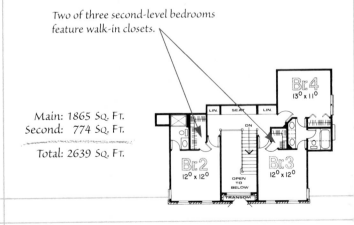

IMPRESSIONS - Homes designed for the way you live

Cordeaux

#48B-2174 *Price Code* A27

The kitchen is made more efficient through a walk-in pantry and island counter.

With tall windows and a fireplace, both sides of this family room will be enjoyed.

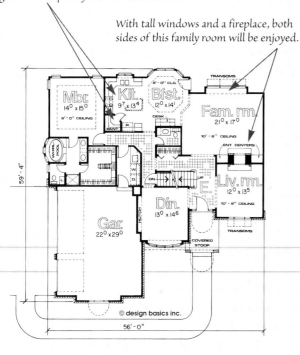

© design basics inc.

56'- 0"

This walk-in linen closet is a great place for storage of extra bedding or children's games.

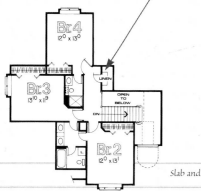

Main: 1860 SQ. FT.
Second: 848 SQ. FT.

Total: 2708 SQ. FT.

Slab and Basement Foundation Plans Included.

Calabretta

#48B-4106 *Price Code* A26

Slab and Basement Foundation Plans Included.

Main: 1333 SQ. FT.
Second: 1280 SQ. FT.

Total: 2613 SQ. FT.

NOTE: 9 ft. main level walls

A built-in seat and wet bar make sense for entertaining in this home.

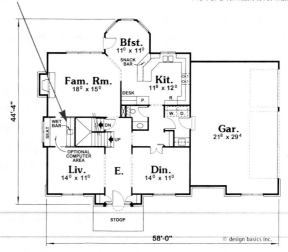

© design basics inc.

58'-0"

In the master suite, a whirlpool tub under a cathedral ceiling and his and her walk-in closets are among an array of amenities.

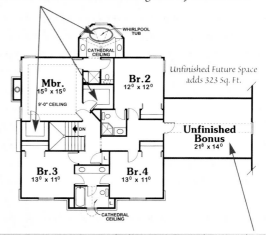

Unfinished Future Space adds 323 Sq. Ft.

The bonus room on the upper level will be nice for homeowners' changing needs.

DESIGN OPTION #3

A. THE CREIGHTON
B. THE KENSINGTON
C. THE EASTGATE

THINK ABOUT...
PORCHES

When most people think about a porch, they think of the deep wrap-around porch of a Queen Anne or of the prominent columns on a Southern Colonial. But porches are much more than these images, and they certainly aren't limited to the front of a home. When considering a porch on your home, think about its many functions: outdoor living space, a quiet retreat, a place to entertain, or a place to grow and display greenery. Porches needn't be large or prominently displayed. They just need to serve a purpose.

3 PERSPECTIVES...

A. The porches in the Creighton function in two ways. First, the smaller rear porch acts as a companion to the breakfast area and is a natural place to grill out. The larger porch becomes an extension of the great room and is perfect for outdoor entertaining.

B. The Kensington is reminiscent of Victorian architecture and features a porch with an angled entry and room for a couple of chairs. This porch was meant for those who desire a porch as outdoor living space.

C. The Eastgate is a perfect example of a home you wouldn't typically expect to have a porch. Yet, a porch was included as a private retreat off the master suite. It's a great place to get away from it all and is the perfect addition to this pampering master bath.

A. Creighton

#48B-4208   Price Code A20

2057 Finished Sq. Ft.

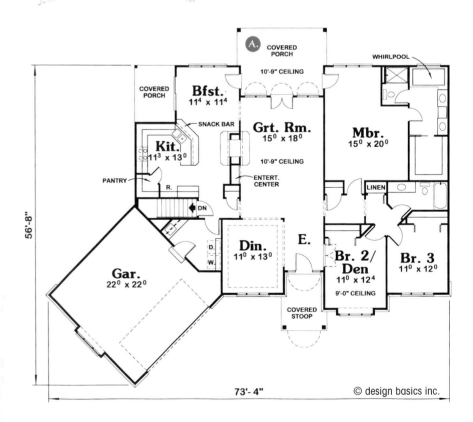

B. Kensington

Main: 1553 Sq. Ft.
Second: 725 Sq. Ft.

Total: 2278 Sq. Ft.

#48B-1864   Price Code A22

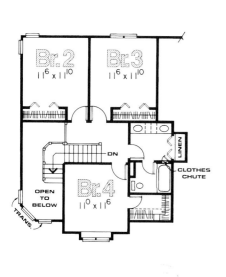

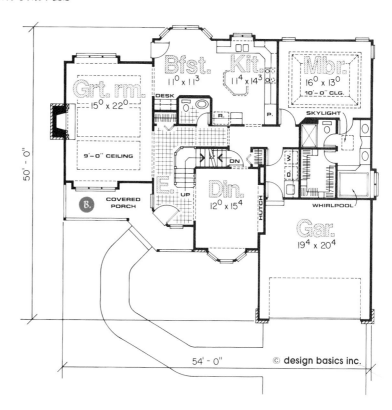

C. Eastgate

#48B-2406   *Price Code A38*

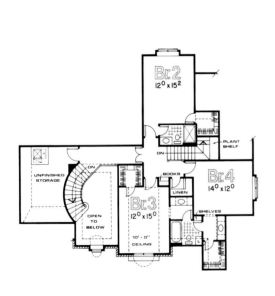

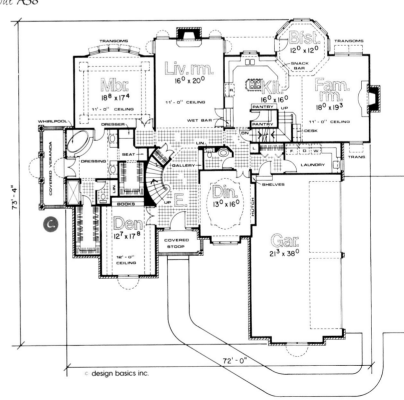

Main: 2789 Sq. Ft.
Second: 1038 Sq. Ft.

Total: 3827 Sq. Ft.

#48B-24007   *Price Code* A29

#48B-24006   *Price Code* A28

Fenwick

The open kitchen, family room and breakfast area make it easy for a family to be together while involved in separate activities.

Storage space given to the garage will be appreciated for lawn and garden equipment.

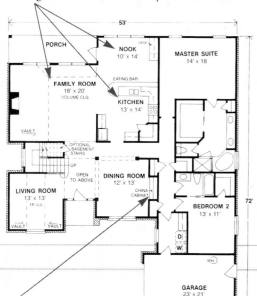

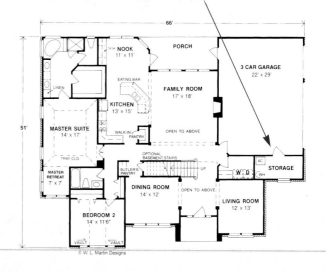

A built-in china cabinet in the formal dining room provides a place for displaying dishes and collectibles.

A second-floor catwalk has a dramatic view into the two-story entry and family room.

Main: 2101 Sq. Ft.
Second: 877 Sq. Ft.

Total: 2978 Sq. Ft.

NOTE: 9 ft. main level walls

Slab, Crawlspace and Basement Foundation Plans Included.

The children will have a place of their own in this second-level game room.

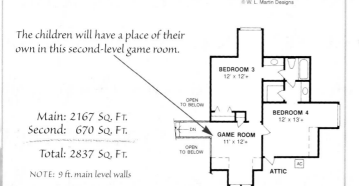

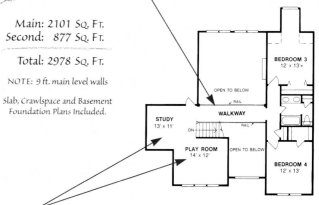

Main: 2167 Sq. Ft.
Second: 670 Sq. Ft.

Total: 2837 Sq. Ft.

NOTE: 9 ft. main level walls

Slab, Crawlspace and Basement Foundation Plans Included.

Whether studying or playing games, the children will enjoy the open study and play room on the second level.

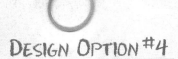

DESIGN OPTION #4

A. THE CARLTON
B. THE CIMMERON
C. THE BETHANY

THINK ABOUT...
ENTRIES

The entry is the true threshold of the home. Since it is the one area of the home guests and strangers alike will inevitably see, it shouldn't be overlooked when selecting a design. Of course, everyone wants the first impressions of their home to be good, but not everyone has the need or budget for an interior water fountain display. Views are key in an entry, whether it be a long view out the back or an interesting stairway. Two-story entries can add a feeling of spaciousness. A view of an elegant dining room set can take the focus off a less than desirable object, such as a closet door. Think about whether or not the entry you select has a view, and whether or not it suits your lifestyle.

3 PERSPECTIVES...

A. The Southern Colonial style of the Carlton, seems appropriately designed with a grand entry. Formal rooms are located on either side of the two-story entry, which views a T-shape stairway. Guests will enjoy this view again and again.

B. The Cimmeron features a long view from the entry through its great room. This design provides secondary views such as arched openings to the living room and a U-shape stairway.

C. The Bethany relies on a vertical view to offer impact. It's U-shape stairway leads to a second-level balcony that overlooks the entry. It provides just enough visual appeal to create warmth upon entering.

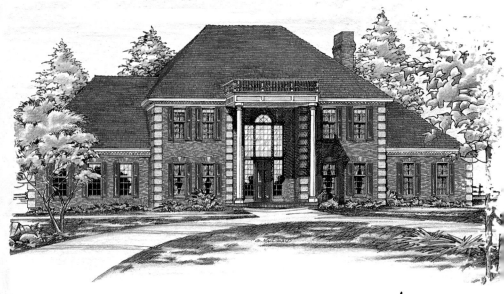

A. Carlton

#48B-1588   Price Code A34

Main: 2500 SQ. FT.
Second: 973 SQ. FT.

Total: 3473 SQ. FT.

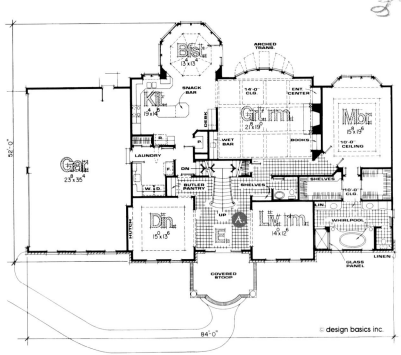

B. Cimmeron

#48B-2215   *Price Code* A28

Main: 1520 Sq. Ft.
Second: 1334 Sq. Ft.

Total: 2854 Sq. Ft.

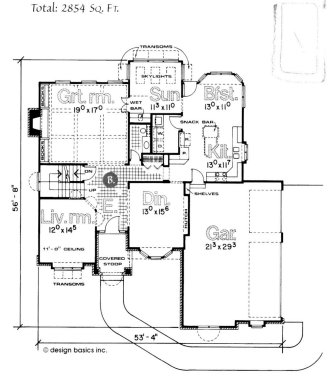

C. Bethany

#48B-3123   *Price Code* A15

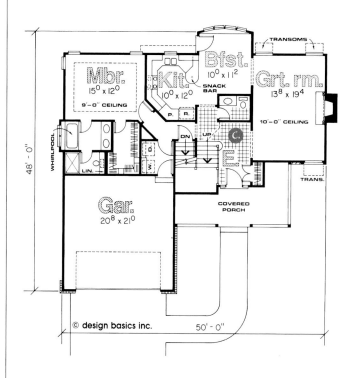

© design basics inc.

50' - 0"

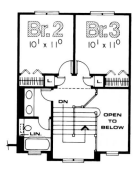

Main: 1191 Sq. Ft.
Second: 405 Sq. Ft.

Total: 1596 Sq. Ft.

DESIGN OPTION #5

A. THE HARTMAN
B. THE AINSLEY
C. THE REMINGTON

THINK ABOUT...
FORMAL LIVING AREAS

Even though today's lifestyles seem to be getting increasingly casual, many of us still have the need for formal living spaces within a home. When considering formal areas, think about your needs. Perhaps you entertain clients, desire a place for eating on formal occasions or just have need for a place to put the piano or dining room furniture. If you include more than one formal room in the selection of your home, keep in mind the relationship between the rooms. Traffic flow should be comfortable and stem from a natural progression between dining and relaxation.

3 PERSPECTIVES...

A. In the Hartman, the formal living and dining rooms are positioned to the left of the entry and flow into each other. This relationship not only provides a long view when in either room, it is also ideal for comfortable traffic flow as guests intermingle.

B. An open staircase becomes a part of the impact of the formal rooms in the Ainsley. Flanking the entry, the formal rooms allow guests immediate access as they enter the home. A serving counter also offers convenience when serving meals in the dining room.

C. Double doors offer seclusion to the formal rooms in the Remington. The living room features built-in shelves and a view to the front through an arched window. The kitchen stays out of view from the dining room, positioned just across the hall from the living room.

A. Hartman

#48B-3333   *Price Code* A23

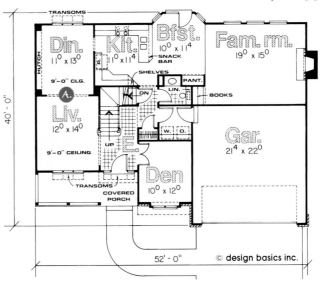

Main: 1273 SQ. FT.
Second: 1035 SQ. FT.

Total: 2308 SQ. FT.

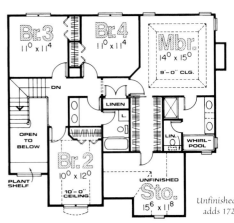

Unfinished Storage adds 172 Sq. Ft.

IMPRESSIONS— *Homes designed for the way you live*

B. Ainsley

#48B-4145   Price Code A23

Main: 1214 Sq. Ft.
Second: 1118 Sq. Ft.

Total: 2332 Sq. Ft.

NOTE: 9 ft. main level walls

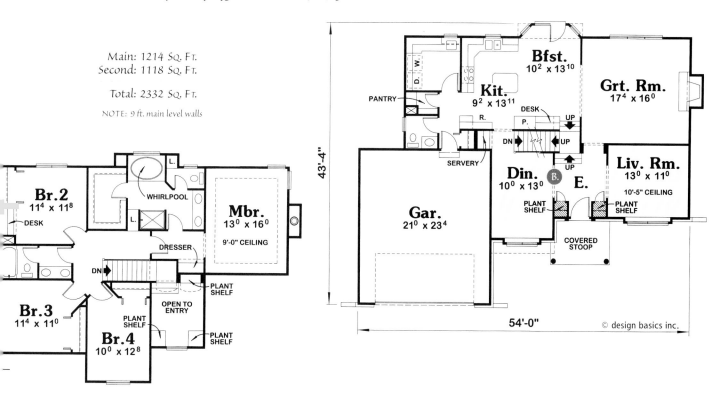

C. Remington

#48B-1486   *Price Code A28*

Main: 1972 Sq. Ft.
Second: 893 Sq. Ft.

Total: 2865 Sq. Ft.

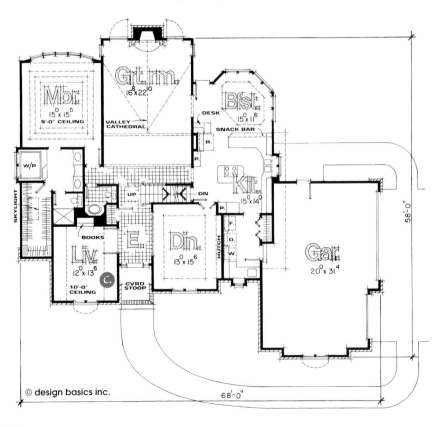

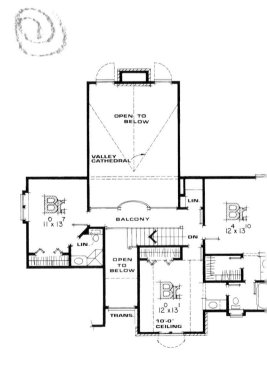

© design basics inc.

68'-0"

BUILT BY: Landmark Homes

Laramy

#48B-3555 *Price Code* A15

BUILT BY: Cannon Construction

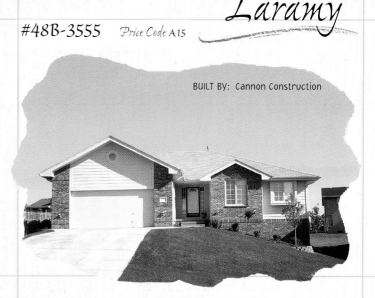

Kaplin

#48B-1963 *Price Code* A13

Secluded for privacy, the master suite has a large window to take advantage of an inviting view to the back.

With access off the breakfast area, this covered porch is the ideal place to grill outdoors.

The family room is symmetrically designed with a cathedral ceiling, tall windows and a central fireplace.

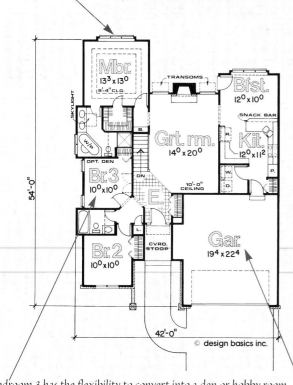

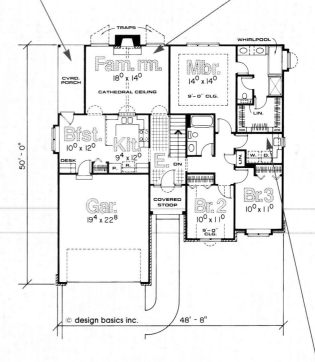

edroom 3 has the flexibility to convert into a den or hobby room.

Extra space in this garage leaves plenty of room for a garden center or work bench.

The laundry room's location in the bedroom wing streamlines this household chore.

1518 Finished Sq. Ft.

1347 Finished Sq. Ft.

Slab and Basement Foundation Plans Included.

design basics inc.
HOME PLAN DESIGN SERVICE

HOME OWNER IMPRESSIONS

ON LIVING IN THE BRITTANY

Most people who build a new home will never get the luxury of hearing coyotes or of getting a view of a starry night. But for David and Kathy, and their four children, these are everyday occurrences of their life in the country.

It could have been that the cramped living quarters in their previous home caused them to feel as though everything was closing in on them.

It could have been the fact that Kathy had grown up in a rural area and missed the wide open spaces. It could have been the illusion - or even the bonafide fact - that life slows down in the country. But whatever the reason that drove them there, Dave and Kathy wouldn't choose to live anywhere else.

"When we decided to build, we started looking at lots in the town where we previously lived, but decided that the homes were just too close together for us. That's when we started looking in the country," David says.

Their search eventually brought them to the three-acre lot where their home, Design Basics'"Brittany", now sits. An important consideration for the family was that their home would take advantage of their rural views.

"The great room was one of the first things that drew us to the plan. It has a window to the front and out the back," Kathy says. "Because of the view out here, we felt that was a desirable aspect to this home."

Another design aspect right at home in the country is its front, wrap-around porch. Both David and Kathy

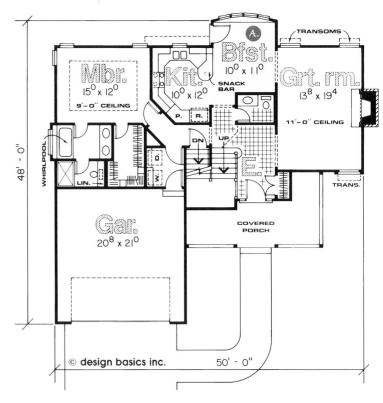

continued on page 24

A. *Brittany*

#48B-3385 *Price Code* A17

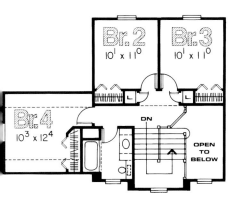

Br. 2
10¹ x 11⁰

Br. 3
10¹ x 11⁰

Br. 4
10³ x 12⁴

DN

OPEN
TO
BELOW

Main: 1191 Sq. Ft.
Second: 597 Sq. Ft.

Total: 1788 Sq. Ft.

Slab and Basement Foundation Plans Included.

THINK ABOUT...
KITCHEN AMENITIES

While kitchens today serve a variety of functions - from entertaining to bill paying - they're still the place where cooking and serving are carried out. When selecting the amenities, give yourself features that will make your work there convenient: a snack bar for serving or a quick meal, an island counter, a sink with a view, a large pantry for storage. Think about how you use this area and what would be best for your needs. And remember, even though kitchens serve a functional need, they can also serve to beautify your home through choice of flooring, countertop material and the latest in cabinet design.

3 PERSPECTIVES...

A. Though the Brittany is smaller in size, its kitchen takes advantage of all available space. An angled pantry offers extra room for storage and a corner snack bar is the perfect place to set out treats for the family.

B. In a larger home such as the Abbey, a large island includes plenty of room for food preparation and features a salad sink. This kitchen also features a planning desk, pantry and view to the back through the nearby open breakfast area.

C. While not solely a kitchen amenity, it is still certainly pleasurable to view a see-through fireplace in the Yorke's kitchen. An island counter is a great feature and forms a working triangle between the stove and sink.

like spending time on the front porch, as well as the deck they added at the back of the home.

David and Kathy finished a walk-out basement on the home, including a family room, bedroom, office and full bath in the lower level. Because of this, they say the home lives much larger than its 1788 square feet and allows each of their children a bedroom of their own.

One area of the home that continues to impress guests, according to Kathy, is the Brittany's two-story entry with U-shape staircase that leads to an upper-level balcony.

"I always get a lot of compliments from people about how appealing it is right when you walk in," Kathy said.

They also desired a home plan that would function for their needs today, as well as in the future.

"Early on we decided that we wanted a home plan that had the master suite on the main floor, allowing us to function on the main level, even after the kids are gone," David says.

Living in the country has not altered Dave and Kathy's viewpoint about living near the conveniences of the big city.

"We appreciate the fact that every day we come home to a completely different environment from where we work," Kathy said. They also appreciate those things the city can never give: A view of rolling hills. A night of stars. The howl of a coyote.

B. Abbey

#48B- 1510   *Price Code* A33

© design basics inc.

Main: 1709 Sq. Ft.
Second: 1597 Sq. Ft.

Total: 3306 Sq. Ft.

C. Yorke

#48B-2217   *Price Code* A20

Main: 1062 Sq. Ft.
Second: 1023 Sq. Ft.

Total: 2085 Sq. Ft.

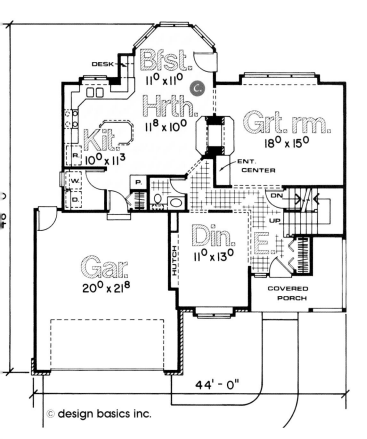

Bfst. 11⁰ x 11⁰
DESK
Hrth. 11⁸ x 10⁰
Kit. 10⁰ x 11³
Grt. rm. 18⁰ x 15⁰
ENT. CENTER
DN
UP
Din. 11⁰ x 13⁰
COVERED PORCH
Gar. 20⁰ x 21⁸
HUTCH
46'
44' - 0"

© design basics inc.

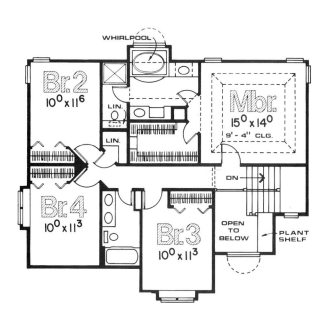

WHIRLPOOL
Br. 2 10⁰ x 11⁶
Mbr. 15⁰ x 14⁰ 9'-4" CLG.
LIN.
LIN.
DN
Br. 4 10⁰ x 11³
Br. 3 10⁰ x 11³
OPEN TO BELOW
PLANT SHELF

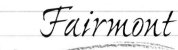

#48B-5519   *Price Code* A 24

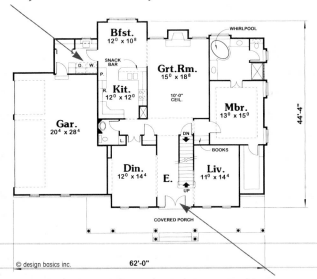

Jennys Brook

#48B-8016   *Price Code* A 16

Bay windows in the breakfast area allow one to take in the view while enjoying a meal.

This great room is the central hub of this home, directing traffic to the kitchen and sleeping areas.

Both a hanging closet and a soaking sink bring functionality to this main-level laundry room.

Bfst.
11^3 x 11^8

Mbr.
13^0 x 15^5

SNACK BAR

Kit.
11^3 x 10^0

Grt. rm.
14^4 x 21^0

Br. 3
11^8 x 10^5

10'-0" CEILING

Br. 2
11^8 x 10^5

Din.
11^4 x 12^5

E.

Gar.
21^0 x 21^8

9'-0" CEILING

COVERED PORCH

© design basics inc.

54' - 0"

54' - 0"

Separate bedroom wings offer privacy for all members of the household.

1691 Finished Sq. Ft.

Slab and Basement Foundation Plans Included.

Bfst.
12^0 x 10^8

WHIRLPOOL

SNACK BAR

Grt.Rm.
15^0 x 18^8

Kit.
12^0 x 12^0

10'-0" CEIL.

Mbr.
13^0 x 15^0

Gar.
20^4 x 28^4

DN

BOOKS

Din.
12^0 x 14^4

E.

Liv.
11^0 x 14^4

UP

© design basics inc.

62'-0"

44'-4"

COVERED PORCH

The impact of this home is emphasized through its French doors that open to the two-story entry.

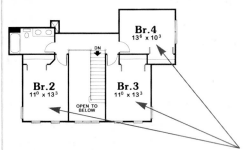

Br.4
13^6 x 10^3

DN

Br.2
11^0 x 13^3

Br.3
11^0 x 13^3

OPEN TO BELOW

Spacious second-level bedrooms will easily accommodate a toy chest or desk.

Main: 1755 Sq. Ft.
Second: 693 Sq. Ft.

Total: 2448 Sq. Ft.

NOTE: 9 ft. main level walls

#48B-1019 *Price Code A22*

Arbor

#48B-2526 *Price Code A16*

The kitchen is strategically placed near both eating areas.

This island counter forms an efficient working triangle between the sink and stove.

Front and rear views are given extra emphasis in the great room through transom windows.

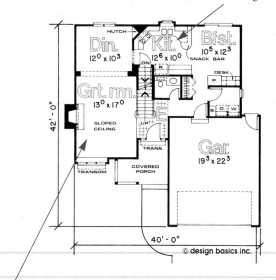

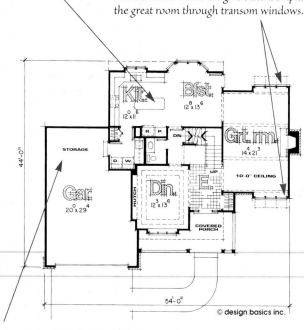

This two-story great room brings a sense of spaciousness to this efficient home.

The garage offers plenty of storage space for lawn and garden equipment.

An upper-level balcony overlooks the entry and accesses double doors into the master suite.

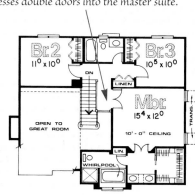

Main: 845 Sq. Ft.
Second: 760 Sq. Ft.

Total: 1605 Sq. Ft.

Main: 1132 Sq. Ft.
Second: 1087 Sq. Ft.

Total: 2219 Sq. Ft.

Slab and Basement Foundation Plans Included.

Design Basics inc.
HOME PLAN DESIGN SERVICE

DESIGN OPTION #7

A. THE NEWMAN
B. THE BRENTWOOD
C. THE EDGEWATER COURT

THINK ABOUT...
INTERIOR VIEWS

One of the easiest ways to enhance your home's overall appeal is to select a floor plan with interior views. Room-to-room views in your home can provide both a feeling of spaciousness and comfort. When considering floor plans, pay attention to the view from the entry. Is there a focal point, a long view or merely dead space? Does each living area of the home visually connect with at least one other area or appealing element within the home? Interior views can open up dead spaces and make you and your guests feel more at home.

3 PERSPECTIVES...

A. The overall design of the Newman creates spectacular views from the moment of entry. The great room grants a view past a covered deck and to an angled kitchen. The dining room is also a focal point in this home with its unusual shape.

B. The dining room, arched windows in the great room and a see-through fireplace are all elements that provide impact from the entry of the Brentwood. Informal views in the hearth room take on a circular pattern, mingling with the kitchen and dinette.

C. The entry in the Edgewater Court immediately catches view of a U-shape stairway and also passes through the family room to the back. The family and dining rooms also have view of each other through arched openings.

A. Newman

#48B-1689   Price Code A21

2133 Finished Sq. Ft.

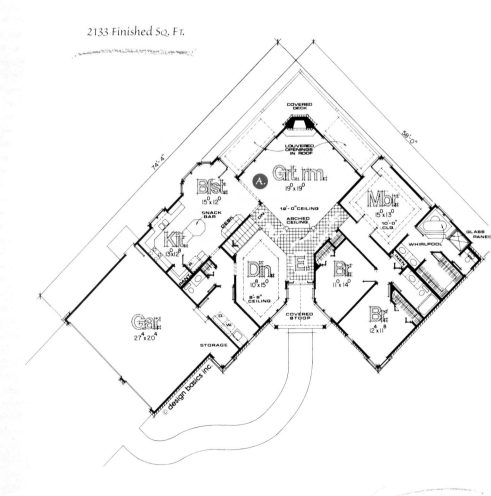

28

B. Brentwood

#48B-3598   Price Code A21

Mbr.
14⁰ x 15⁰
9'-0" CEILING

COVERED DECK

WHIRLPOOL

Grt. rm.
18⁰ x 15⁰
10'-0" CEILING

ENT. CENTER

Bfst.
11⁰ x 11⁰

SNACK BAR

Kit.
11⁰ x 13²

Hrth.
11⁰ x 15⁰

P.   R.

B.

LIN.

WET BAR

LIN.

W.   D.

Br. 3
11⁰ x 12⁰

Br. 2
11⁴ x 12⁰
10'-6" CEILING
OPTIONAL DEN

LIN.

Din.
11⁴ x 15⁰
10'-0" CLG.

DN

COVERED PORCH

Gar.
22⁰ x 31⁸

© design basics inc.

64' - 0"

BOOKS

Den
11⁴ x 13⁰
10'-6" CEILING

OPTIONAL DEN

2187 Finished Sq. Ft.

Slab and Basement Foundation Plans Included.

C. Edgewater Court

#48B-9159   Price Code B24

2409 Finished Sq. Ft.

Slab and Basement Foundation Plans Included.

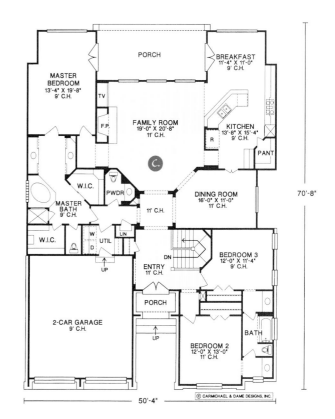

PORCH

MASTER BEDROOM
13'-4" X 19'-8"
9' C.H.

TV

F.P.

FAMILY ROOM
19'-0" X 20'-8"
11' C.H.

BREAKFAST
11'-4" X 11'-0"
9' C.H.

KITCHEN
13'-8" X 15'-4"
9' C.H.

PANT.

R.

W.I.C.

PWDR

C.

11' C.H.

DINING ROOM
16'-0" X 11'-0"
11' C.H.

70'-8"

MASTER BATH
9' C.H.

W.I.C.

W   D   UTIL   LIN

UP

DN

ENTRY
11' C.H.

BEDROOM 3
12'-0" X 11'-4"
9' C.H.

2-CAR GARAGE
9' C.H.

PORCH

UP

BEDROOM 2
12'-0" X 13'-0"
11' C.H.

BATH

50'-4"

© CARMICHAEL & DAME DESIGNS, INC.

DESIGN OPTION #8

A. THE MONTE VISTA
B. THE ALLISTON
C. THE CLARIDGE HOUSE

THINK ABOUT...
KITCHEN LOCATION

The kitchen is often identified as the "heart" of a home. It seems to be the place where all naturally congregate. Whatever the reason for this, it is a fact that the kitchen's role within a home will always be important. Among the cabinet and amenity selections that will inevitably go along with the design of your kitchen, don't overlook its location. Think about whether you want an open view of your kitchen, or whether you'd rather have it more secluded in case of dishes that may pile up. Perhaps you wish the kitchen to truly become an entertaining area. Its proper location will secure its pleasure within your home.

3 PERSPECTIVES...

A. In the Monte Vista, the kitchen is designed in a central location. This serves a variety of functions, as it is accessible from the breakfast area, dining room and great room.

B. The kitchen in the Alliston is designed to openly share space within the informal areas of the home. It is located for privacy from view of the entry, but still is integrated with the living areas.

C. The frontal position of the kitchen in the Claridge House is not often seen, but here it is ideal for its close proximity to the garage and dining room. It also allows the living and family rooms to take advantage of rear locations to optimize views to the back.

A. Monte Vista

#48B-1032   *Price Code* A16

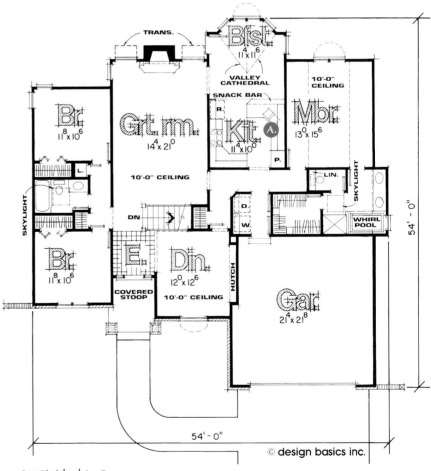

1697 Finished Sq. Ft.

© design basics inc.

B. Alliston

#48B-5497   *Price Code* A23

Main: 1256 SQ. FT.
Second: 1108 SQ. FT.

Total: 2364 SQ. FT.

NOTE: 9 ft. main level walls

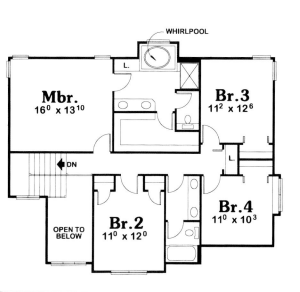

WHIRLPOOL

Mbr.
16⁰ x 13¹⁰

Br.3
11² x 12⁶

DN

OPEN TO
BELOW

Br.2
11⁰ x 12⁰

Br.4
11⁰ x 10³

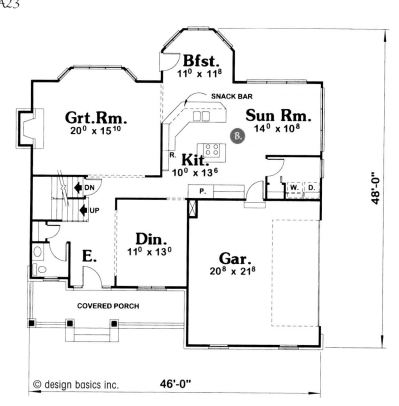

Bfst.
11⁰ x 11⁸

SNACK BAR

Grt.Rm.
20⁰ x 15¹⁰

Sun Rm.
14⁰ x 10⁸

B.

R.   **Kit.**
10⁰ x 13⁶

DN
UP

P.   W. D.

Din.
11⁰ x 13⁰

E.

Gar.
20⁸ x 21⁸

COVERED PORCH

48'-0"

© design basics inc.   46'-0"

C. Claridge House

#48B-9157   *Price Code* B35

Main: 2050 Sq. Ft.
Second: 1467 Sq. Ft.

Total: 3517 Sq. Ft.

Slab and Basement Foundation Plans Included.

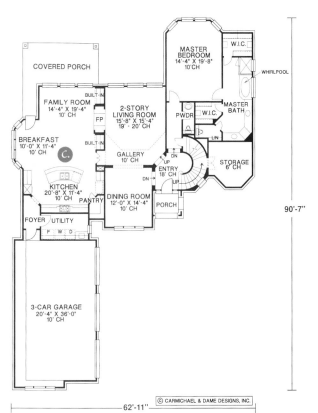

COVERED PORCH

FAMILY ROOM
14'-4" X 19'-4"
10' CH

BUILT-IN

2-STORY
LIVING ROOM
15'-8" X 15'-4"
19' - 20' CH

MASTER
BEDROOM
14'-4" X 19'-8"
10' CH

W.I.C.

WHIRLPOOL

FP

BUILT-IN

BREAKFAST
10'-0" X 11'-4"
10' CH

PWDR

W.I.C.

MASTER
BATH

GALLERY
10' CH

LIN

KITCHEN
20'-8" X 11'-4"
10' CH

PANTRY

DINING ROOM
12'-0" X 14'-4"
10' CH

DN
UP
ENTRY
18' CH
DN
UP

STORAGE
6' CH

FOYER / UTILITY

PORCH

F W D

3-CAR GARAGE
20'-4" X 36'-0"
10' CH

90'-7"

62'-11"

© CARMICHAEL & DAME DESIGNS, INC.

BEDROOM 2
14'-4" X 14'-0"
8'-10" CH

LIN

BEDROOM 3
14'-0" X 13'-4"
11' CH

BUILT-INS

W.I.C.

2-STORY
LIVING ROOM

BATH

W.I.C.

BEDROOM 5
12'-4" X 12'-0"
8' CH

W.I.C.

BALCONY
8' CH

DN

BATH

OPEN
TO
BELOW

BUILT-INS

STUDY
11'-0" X 11'-0"
13' CH

W.I.C.

BEDROOM 4
12'-0" X 14'-4"
10' CH

IMPRESSIONS– *Homes designed for the way you live*

BUILT BY: Dan Lowe Construction

PHOTO BY: Phil Bell

Marcell

#48B-4133   *Price Code* A17

A compartmentalized bath allows more than one to get ready in the master bath.

Triple-arched windows and a fireplace provide the great room three focal points to enjoy.

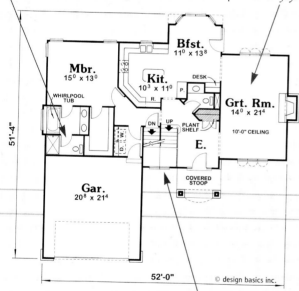

Mbr. 15⁰ x 13⁰

WHIRLPOOL TUB

Kit. 10³ x 11⁰

Bfst. 11⁰ x 13⁸

DESK

P

R

UP

DN

PLANT SHELF

E.

Grt. Rm. 14⁰ x 21⁴

10'-0" CEILING

51'-4"

Gar. 20⁸ x 21⁴

COVERED STOOP

52'-0"

© design basics inc.

A window lights the stairway, as well as the two-story entry.

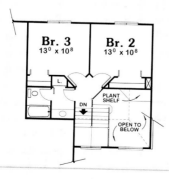

Br. 3 13⁰ x 10⁸

Br. 2 13⁰ x 10⁸

L

DN

PLANT SHELF

OPEN TO BELOW

Main: 1314 SQ. FT.
Second: 458 SQ. FT.

Total: 1772 SQ. FT.

NOTE: 8 ft. main level walls

#48B-3249   *Price Code* A22

Tanner

BUILT BY: Bill Branz Building & Remodeling

A see-through fireplace makes a great centerpiece between the breakfast area and great room.

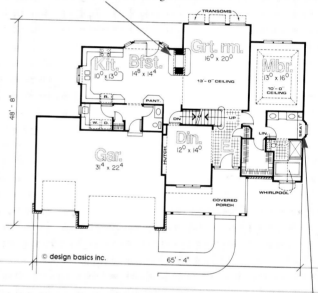

TRANSOMS

Kit. 10⁰ x 13⁰

Bfst. 14⁸ x 14⁴

Grt. rm. 16⁰ x 20⁰

13'-0" CEILING

R

PANT.

W. D.

DN

UP

Mbr. 13⁰ x 16⁰

10'-0" CEILING

LIN.

SEAT

48'-8"

Gar. 31⁴ x 22⁴

HUTCH

Din. 12⁰ x 14⁰

E.

WHIRLPOOL

COVERED PORCH

© design basics inc.

65'-4"

A built-in window seat in the master bath is a nice accompaniment to a double vanity with make-up counter.

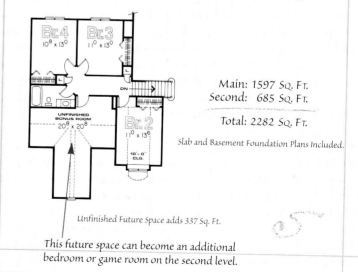

Br. 4 10⁸ x 13⁰

Br. 3 11⁰ x 13⁰

L

L

DN

UNFINISHED BONUS ROOM 20⁸ x 20⁸

Br. 2 11⁰ x 13⁶

10'-0" CLG.

Main: 1597 SQ. FT.
Second: 685 SQ. FT.

Total: 2282 SQ. FT.

Slab and Basement Foundation Plans Included.

Unfinished Future Space adds 337 Sq. Ft.

This future space can become an additional bedroom or game room on the second level.

DESIGN OPTION #9

A. THE COLLINS FALLS
B. THE PINNACLE
C. THE LEAWOOD

THINK ABOUT...
HOME OFFICES

On the rise in this country are the number of individuals who work from home. While you may not be one of them, you may still require a place within your home to complete work you've brought home from the office, pay household bills or organize your agenda for the day. If considering a home office as you select your floor plan, think about the location that would be most appropriate for you. The size and amenities in your home office should also correspond with your needs, such as a built-in desk or shelves or dramatic windows and double doors to provide impact if in a prominent location.

3 PERSPECTIVES...

A. The Collins Falls offers the perfect opportunity to adapt the home for a future home office. Bedroom 2 can be converted into a den with double doors off the bedroom hall.

B. With double doors off the entry, the den in the Pinnacle is a great location for someone working out of their home. It features a front view and allows guests or clients easy access.

C. The den in the Leawood, has a somewhat more secluded location. It can also serve as a second living area with dramatic features such as tall windows with transoms and a spider-beam ceiling.

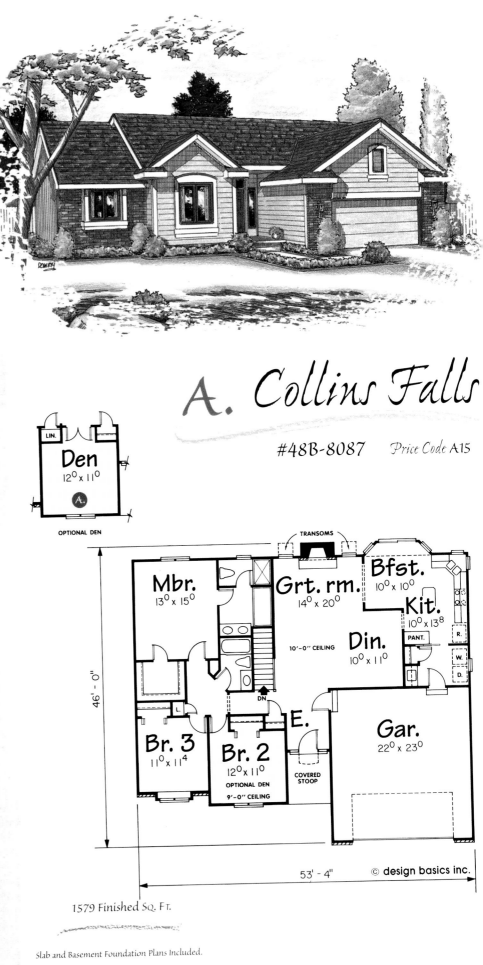

A. Collins Falls

#48B-8087   *Price Code* A15

Den 12⁰ x 11⁰

OPTIONAL DEN

1579 Finished Sq. Ft.

Slab and Basement Foundation Plans Included.

IMPRESSIONS– *Homes designed for the way you live*

B. *Pinnacle*

#48B-3284 *Price Code* A24

© design basics inc.

Main: 1777 SQ. FT.
Second: 719 SQ. FT.

Total: 2496 SQ. FT.

Slab and Basement Foundation Plans Included.

C. *Leawood*

#48B-2779 *Price Code* A26

© design basics inc.

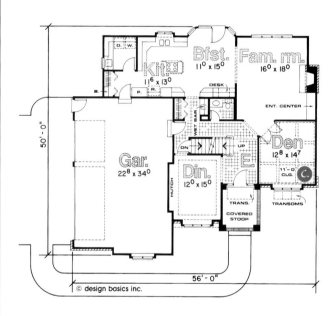

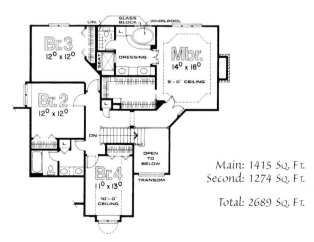

Main: 1415 SQ. FT.
Second: 1274 SQ. FT.

Total: 2689 SQ. FT.

#48B-8028   *Price Code* A16

Leighton

#48B-2377   *Price Code* A16

Built-in bookshelves near the master suite are a great place to display family photos.

Wrapping counters create increased efficiency while cooking and preparing meals in this kitchen.

Bayed windows will not only bring in a lot of light to the breakfast area, but that light will also extend into the kitchen.

The dining room is really flexible in this home, allowing expansion from the great room.

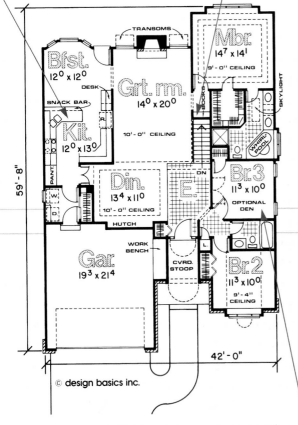

© design basics inc.

Bedroom 3 suggests conversion into a home office or den for the work-at-home professional.

1636 Finished Sq. Ft.

Slab and Basement Foundation Plans Included.

This upper-level storage area has so many uses. It can expand the master suite's walk-in closet or be incorporated into a nursery.

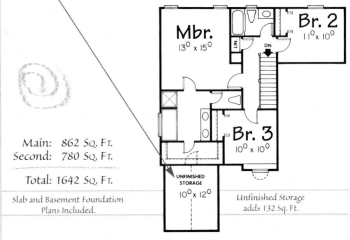

Main: 862 Sq. Ft.
Second: 780 Sq. Ft.

Total: 1642 Sq. Ft.

Slab and Basement Foundation Plans Included.

Unfinished Storage adds 132 Sq. Ft.

IMPRESSIONS– *Homes designed for the way you live*

Juniper

#48B-2308   *Price Code* A17

Stevens Woods

#48B-8053   *Price Code* A19

The master suite has everything that's needed - along with the luxury of a triple window and corner garden tub.

Because of tall, bay windows, both the great room and breakfast area will receive a lot of light.

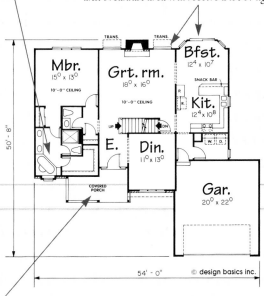

Mbr.
15⁰ x 13⁰
10'-0" CEILING

Grt. rm.
18⁰ x 16⁰
10'-0" CEILING

Bfst.
12⁴ x 10⁷

SNACK BAR

Kit.
12⁴ x 10⁸

E.

Din.
11⁰ x 13⁰

Gar.
20⁰ x 22⁰

COVERED PORCH

50'-8"

54'-0"

© design basics inc.

The front porch seems to be meant for solitude, with room for a comfortable chair.

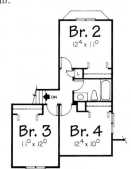

Br. 2
12⁴ x 11⁰

Br. 3
11⁰ x 12⁰

Br. 4
12⁴ x 10⁰

Main: 1398 SQ. FT.
Second: 598 SQ. FT.

Total: 1996 SQ. FT.

This design also features a family room secluded for more private interaction.

An open feeling is generated in this home through a two-story entry and connected living and dining rooms.

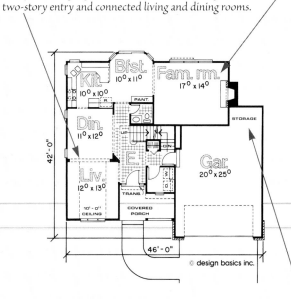

Kit.
10⁰ x 11⁰

Bfst.
10⁰ x 10⁰

Fam. rm.
17⁰ x 14⁰

PANT.

Din.
11⁰ x 12⁰

STORAGE

E.

Gar.
20⁰ x 25⁰

Liv.
12⁰ x 13⁰
10'-0" CEILING

TRANS.

COVERED PORCH

42'-0"

46'-0"

© design basics inc.

Mbr.
13⁰ x 14⁰
8'-8" CEILING

WHIRLPOOL

LIN

DN

Br. 2
11² x 10⁰

OPEN TO BELOW

PLANT SHELF

Br. 3
10⁸ x 10³

Extra storage is provided in the garage and in a walk-in closet in bedroom 2.

Main: 1032 SQ. FT.
Second: 743 SQ. FT.

Total: 1775 SQ. FT.

HOME OWNER IMPRESSIONS
ON LIVING IN THE LINCOLN

THE DEBATE: *Significantly expand their 3-bedroom, 1,200 square-foot one-story home, or for relatively the same price, build a new home.*

Tom and Cindy grappled with this debate for many months. They liked the neighborhood they lived in well enough - but a lot overlooking a golf course was tempting. There wasn't anything wrong with their 23-year-old home, aside from the fact that they were desiring more space. They'd made all the usual updates to the windows, carpets and cabinets in recent years - but a brand new home would erase the need for any updates for a while. Their chosen lot was a rather difficult one to find a design to suit it - but they did find one plan that would work nicely for them...

"In the end, I guess we couldn't turn down the 7 percent interest rates," Tom said. So, Tom and Cindy along with their son, Chris, decided to take the plunge and build a new home. The plan that suited their challenging lot and their living needs was Design Basics' "Lincoln."

"It had to be a smaller house to fit on the lot, but we didn't want a small home. So the design itself ended up being a two-story home so that we could get the added square footage we needed and still have the home fit on the lot," Tom said.

Convenience was a major consideration in selecting a design. And, for Tom and Cindy, that meant the location of the laundry room.

"We wanted it on the same level as the master suite and this particular plan had that option," Cindy said. "It's really

continued on page 40

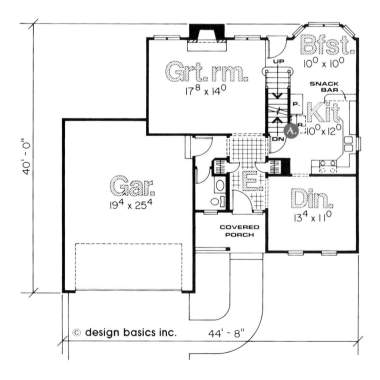

© design basics inc.   44' - 8"

A. THE LINCOLN
B. THE BARRINGTON WOOD
C. THE DEVONSHIRE

THINK ABOUT...
STAIRWAY LOCATION

The position of a staircase should be carefully considered when selecting your floor plan. Most homes, because of square footage considerations, will only have one staircase, so its function and position should be commiserate with your lifestyle. Consider the most logical access point for traffic flow and how it visually corresponds with the design of other living areas.

3 PERSPECTIVES...

A. The staircase in the Lincoln, is located to the rear near the main living areas of the home. It is perfect in this design, since these living areas of the home will most likely be used by the family on a daily basis.

B. The T-shape stairway in the Barrington Wood is an efficient use of space in this home. It provides the visual appeal of a curved stairway in the entry and also functional access to the second level from the utility area and hearth room.

C. Because of the size of the Devonshire, both a front and rear staircase are appropriate in this design. The fanning stairway in the entry serves as a focal point. The rear staircase allows traffic in the kitchen and great room to access the second level without having to enter the formal area of the home.

A. Lincoln

#48B-3097   Price Code A17

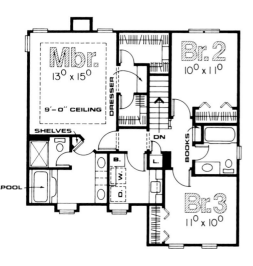

Main: 852 SQ. FT.
Second: 893 SQ. FT.

Total: 1745 SQ. FT.

nice to be able to put in a load of laundry in the morning or evening and not have to travel up and down the stairway."

In the Lincoln, the stairway to the second level is located to the rear of the home, which was also convenience factor for Tom and Cindy.

"Because we are on a golf course, and most of the view is oriented to the back, it's kind of nice to have that be a focal point when we're in the kitchen or family room," Cindy said.

Because this family of three doesn't require a lot of eating space, they made the decision before they built to utilize the dining room as a sitting room - preferring to dine in the casual breakfast area.

But these convenience features only serve to enhance their experience of living in the home. Their "favorite" areas of the home are the kitchen and great room. Besides being able to view the golf course, the two rooms are the hub of family time activity in their home.

"Most evenings that's where we are," Cindy said. " I like the fact that they're all connected. Someone can be in the kitchen, others sitting at the dinette table and some in the great room and we can all still converse with each other."

Other than having to contend with an unwanted golf ball or two, Tom and Cindy say the decision to build the Lincoln has been the right one for them. But just to shake their seemingly peaceful lives in this home, Chris has just graduated from high school and will be attending college in the fall. So that just leaves the two of them. And well, they could use a little bit more space for entertaining and there are some rather interesting lots in the area.

B. *Barrington Wood*

#48B- 1035   *Price Code* A29

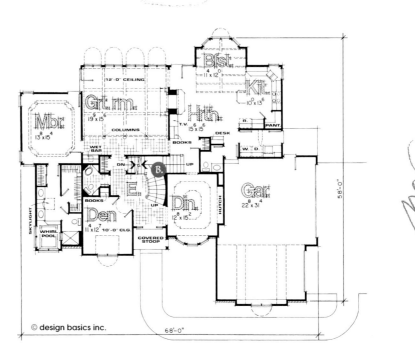

© design basics inc.

Main: 2040 Sq. Ft.
Second: 927 Sq. Ft.

Total: 2967 Sq. Ft.

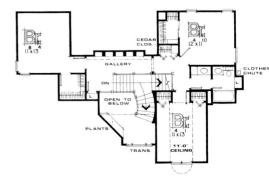

C. Devonshire

#48B-1824   Price Code A31

Main: 2231 Sq. Ft.
Second: 933 Sq. Ft.

Total: 3164 Sq. Ft.

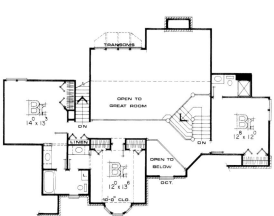

#48B-2246   *Price Code* A17

Kaiser

#48B-2578   *Price Code* A16

The breakfast area is a great intermediary between the kitchen and great room and offers a built-in desk.

Tall transom windows invite natural light into this functional, two-story great room.

A sloped ceiling adds interest to the break-fast area with access to the backyard.

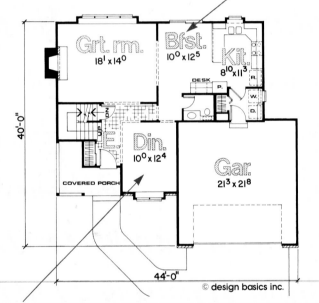

Grt. rm.
18' x 14⁰

Bfst.
10⁰ x 12⁵

Kit.
8¹⁰ x 11³

DESK   P.

40'-0"

UP   Din.
10⁰ x 12⁴

Gar.
21³ x 21⁸

COVERED PORCH

44'-0"

© design basics inc.

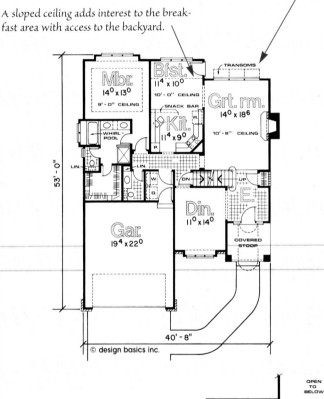

Mbr.
14⁰ x 13⁰
9'-0" ceiling

Bfst.
11⁴ x 10⁰
10'-0" ceiling

TRANSOMS

SNACK BAR

Grt. rm.
14⁰ x 18⁶
10'-8" ceiling

WHIRL-POOL

Kit.
11⁴ x 9⁰   R.

LIN.   LIN.

W   D

DN   UP

Din.
11⁰ x 14⁰

COVERED STOOP

Gar.
19⁴ x 22⁰

53'-0"

40'-8"

© design basics inc.

This dining room takes in a view to the front and of the U-shape stairway.

Main: 891 Sq. Ft.
Second: 885 Sq. Ft.

Total: 1776 Sq. Ft.

Main: 1327 Sq. Ft.
Second: 348 Sq. Ft.

Total: 1675 Sq. Ft.

OPEN TO BELOW

DN

Br. 2
10⁰ x 10⁰

Br. 3
10⁰ x 10⁰

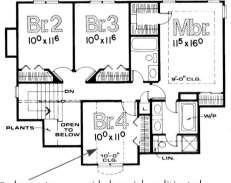

Br. 2
10⁰ x 11⁶

Br. 3
10⁰ x 11⁶

Mbr.
11⁵ x 16⁰
9'-0" CLG.

DN

PLANTS

OPEN TO BELOW

Br. 4
10⁰ x 11⁰
10'-0" CLG.

L   W/P

LIN.

Boxed windows with ledges offer a creative display area for a child's toys.

Bedroom 4 was provided special qualities to be appreciated by guests: a 10-foot ceiling and arched window.

Rosebury

#48B-1767   *Price Code* A16

#48B-2350   *Price Code* A28

Wingate

This family room is given a lot character through several focal points: a tall window, fireplace, French doors and a curved staircase.

The great room will feel more spacious with its cathedral ceiling.

A wet bar/servery is a practical element to help serve meals in the dining room.

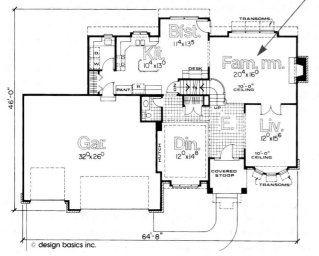

© design basics inc.

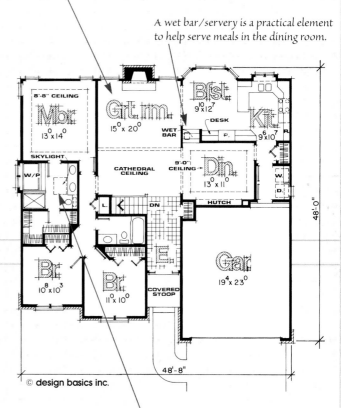

© design basics inc.

The master bath has many conveniences, including his-and-her vanities and a built-in ironing board.

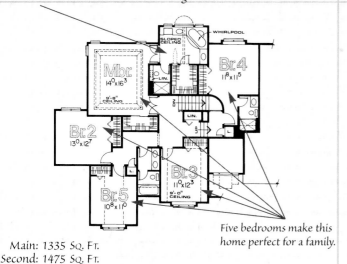

Five bedrooms make this home perfect for a family.

The extra light generated from the skylight above the vanity in the master suite will be appreciated by those getting ready.

Main: 1335 Sq. Ft.
Second: 1475 Sq. Ft.

Total: 2810 Sq. Ft.

1604 Finished Sq. Ft.

Slab and Basement Foundation Plans Included.

design basics inc.
HOME PLAN DESIGN SERVICE

ORDER DIRECT- (800) 947-7526   www.designbasics.com   **43**

Design Option #11

A. The Collier
B. The Aberdeen
C. The Excaliber

Think About...
Master Suite Location

Of the things that we covet most, sleeping is among the most hallowed. We want peace from our day. We want quiet from the noises encroaching upon us. We want, for a mere seven or eight hours, a brief retreat from reality. The master suite will be the only room in the home that is truly yours. And that is why it is important to carefully consider its location within your home. Your desire for seclusion from main-level activity may warrant the master suite on an upper level. Your desire to be close to, or separated from your children may result in completely different scenarios of design. In whatever floor plan you select, the location of the master suite - your one true haven - should not be overlooked.

3 Perspectives...

A. Those desiring to be close to their children will benefit from the design of the Collier. All bedrooms are located on the second level and are within steps of each other.

B. In one-story designs, it can be difficult to obtain true seclusion for the master suite. In the Aberdeen, optimal separation was provided by separating the master suite from two secondary bedrooms - each placed to flank the living areas of the home.

C. In the Excalibur, the master suite is a true haven, located midway up the stairway and including a private den. Three other bedrooms are placed on the upper level, at the opposite end of the home.

S. JANICEK

A. Collier

#48B-2216   Price Code A2

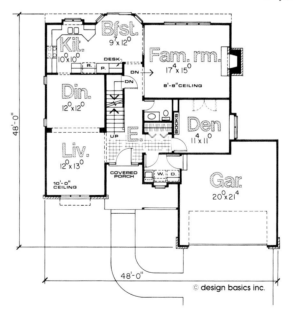

© design basics inc.

Main: 1224 SQ. FT.
Second: 950 SQ. FT.

Total: 2174 SQ. FT.

B. *Aberdeen*

#48B-2321   *Price Code* A22

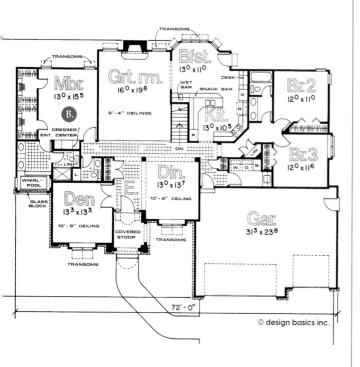

2276 Finished Sq. Ft.

C. *Excalibur*

#48B-3210   *Price Code* A32

Main: 2235 Sq. Ft.
Second: 1003 Sq. Ft.

Total: 3238 Sq. Ft.

Unfinished Future Space
adds 274 Sq. Ft.

BUILT BY: Dennis Smit Construction

Laverton

#48B-2248   *Price Code* A16

The great room is large enough to accommodate many and includes a fireplace and view to the back.

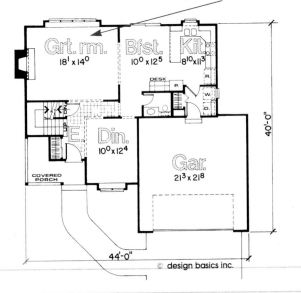

Grt. rm.
18¹ x 14⁰

Bfst.
10⁰ x 12⁵

Kit.
8¹⁰ x 11³

DESK

Din.
10⁰ x 12⁴

Gar.
21³ x 21⁸

COVERED PORCH

40'-0"

44'-0"

© design basics inc.

It's hard not to imagine soaking in this whirlpool resting beneath a double window.

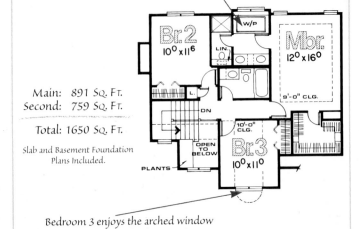

Br. 2
10⁰ x 11⁶

W/P

LIN.

Mbr.
12⁰ x 16⁰

9'-0" CLG.

DN

10'-0" CLG.

OPEN TO BELOW

Br. 3
10⁰ x 11⁰

PLANTS

Main: 891 SQ. FT.
Second: 759 SQ. FT.

Total: 1650 SQ. FT.

Slab and Basement Foundation Plans Included.

Bedroom 3 enjoys the arched window that characterizes this home's elevation.

Jennings

#48B-3246   *Price Code* A26

BUILT BY: Kuszmaul Builders

Double doors serve a functional aspect in the formal rooms.

Enjoy the openness of this kitchen and its view of the see-through fireplace.

Kit.
10⁰ x 14⁰

BOOKS   ENT. CENTER

Bfst.
18⁰ x 13⁰

Fam. rm.
17⁰ x 18⁰

Gar.
20⁸ x 25⁰

HUTCH

Din.
13⁰ x 13⁰

DN

UP

Liv. rm.
12⁰ x 13⁰

COVERED PORCH

42'-0"

© design basics inc.   54'-8"

The master suite has a lot of great amenities, including this walk-in closet with his-and-her compartments.

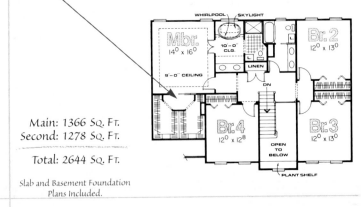

WHIRLPOOL   SKYLIGHT

Mbr.
14⁰ x 16⁰

10'-0" CLG.

9'-0" CEILING

LINEN

Br. 2
12⁰ x 13⁰

DN

Br. 4
12⁰ x 12⁸

OPEN TO BELOW

Br. 3
12⁰ x 13⁰

PLANT SHELF

Main: 1366 SQ. FT.
Second: 1278 SQ. FT.

Total: 2644 SQ. FT.

Slab and Basement Foundation Plans Included.

IMPRESSIONS– Homes designed for the way you live

THINK ABOUT...
ENTERTAINING SPACES

If you are someone who entertains frequently, or who just enjoys throwing parties, then having adequate entertaining space within your new home is a must. For clients or business associates, you may want entertaining areas to be formal. If family and friends are those you entertain, you may want to consider a more casual arrangement for entertaining. Amenities such as serving counters and wet bars can make it easy to serve guests, while open-air porches and patios are great places for guests to enjoy a change of scenery.

3 PERSPECTIVES...

A. Entertaining in the Kendall can be kept strictly to the dining and living rooms for smaller parties. French doors in the living room, however, open to the family room to accommodate larger gatherings.

B. The Sweetwater Bend features open formal rooms sharing a view of the curved staircase and the back. Nearby, walk-up service and butler's bars make ideal buffet counters. And down the hall, a media room provides additional space for guests.

C. A curved wall connects the living and dining rooms in the Edgewood. This home's entertaining space continues through a set of French doors connecting this area to a screened veranda - very desirable during nice weather.

A. Kendall

#48B-1553   *Price Code* A23

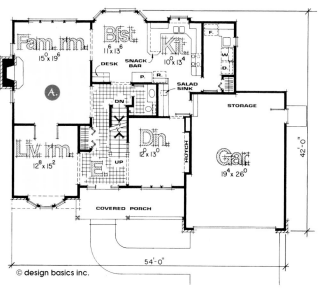

© design basics inc.

Main: 1303 Sq. Ft.
Second: 1084 Sq. Ft.

Total: 2387 Sq. Ft.

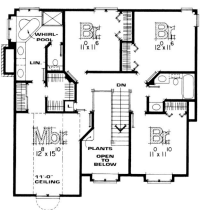

B. Sweetwater Bend

#48B-9119 *Price Code* B42

Main: 2688 SQ. FT.
Second: 1540 SQ. FT.

Total: 4228 SQ. FT.

Slab and Basement Foundation Plans Included.

3 CAR GARAGE
27'-4" X 22'-8"
10' CH

PORCH

UTILITY

MEDIA ROOM
15'-0" X 19'-8"
10' CH

PWDR

WHIRLPOOL

BAR

KITCHEN
14'-0" X 16'-0"
10' CH

LIVING ROOM
18'-8" X 18'-0"
21' CH

MASTER BEDROOM
16'-4" X 18'-0"
10' CH

MASTER BATH

FP

UP

BREAKFAST
10'-8" X 11'-4"
10' CH

BUTLER'S

PANTRY

GALLERY

BUILT-INS

W.I.C.

W.I.C.

UP

STUDY
11'-4" X 11'-4"
10' CH

DINING ROOM
12'-4" X 15'-0"
10' CH

ENTRY

PORCH

© CARMICHAEL & DAME DESIGNS, INC.

80'-1"

84'-3"

ATTIC STORAGE

BUILT-INS

TV

GAME ROOM
15'-0" X 16'-4"
10' CH

DOWN

W.I.C.

BATH

BEDROOM 4
15'-4" X 11'-4"
9' CH

W.I.C.

2-STORY
LIVING ROOM

BEDROOM 2
12'-4" X 16'-4"
9' CH

W.I.C.

BALCONY

BATH

OPEN
TO
BELOW

DOWN

BEDROOM 3
12'-4" X 15'-0"
9' CH

IMPRESSIONS– Homes designed for the way you live

C. Edgewood

#48B-2839   *Price Code A30*

Main: 1631 Sq. Ft.
Second: 1426 Sq. Ft.

Total: 3057 Sq. Ft.

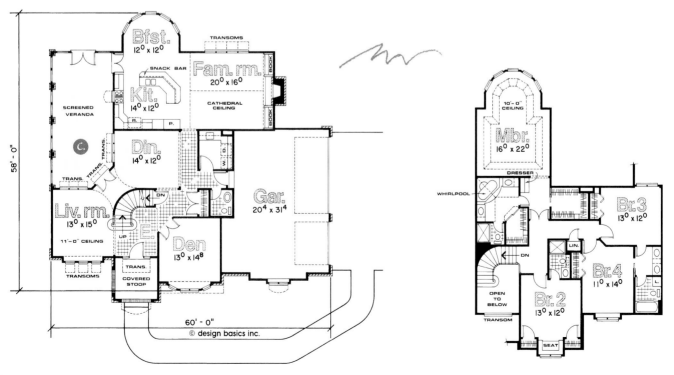

Ackerley

#48B-4642 *Price Code* A17

Ashville

#48B-2811 *Price Code* A22

The front area of this home will be perfect for entertaining, with ideal integration between the front porch, dining room and great room.

Double doors, a sloped, 10-foot ceiling and bay windows result in a memorable breakfast area.

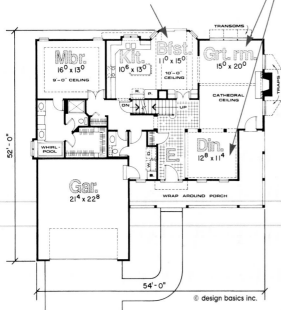

Mbr. 16⁰ x 13⁰ — 9'-0" CEILING
Kit. 10⁶ x 13⁰
Bfst. 11⁰ x 15⁰ — 10'-0" CEILING
Grt. rm. 15⁰ x 20⁰ — CATHEDRAL CEILING
TRANSOMS
Din. 12⁸ x 11⁴
WRAP AROUND PORCH
WHIRLPOOL
Gar. 21⁴ x 22⁸

52'-0"
54'-0"

© design basics inc.

This corridor provides optimal separation to three, second-level bedrooms.

Main: 1570 Sq. Ft.
Second: 707 Sq. Ft.

Total: 2277 Sq. Ft.

Br. 2 12⁰ x 12⁰
Br. 4 12⁰ x 11⁰
Br. 3 12⁰ x 11⁰
OPEN TO BELOW
8'-8" CEILING
PLANT SHELF

Striking interior views into the family room are captured from the breakfast area, stairway and media room.

The flexibility of this media room is so crucial to this home because it can serve so many functions - from eating to office space.

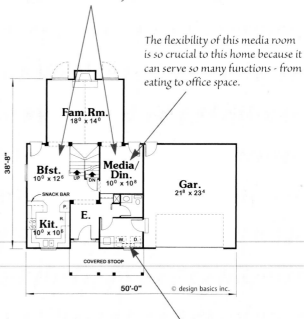

Fam. Rm. 18⁰ x 14⁰
Bfst. 10⁰ x 12⁶
Media/Din. 10⁰ x 10⁸
Gar. 21⁸ x 23⁴
SNACK BAR
Kit. 10⁰ x 10⁸
E.
COVERED STOOP

38'-8"
50'-0"

© design basics inc.

Homeowners will appreciate the space allotted to the laundry room and features such as a window and soaking sink.

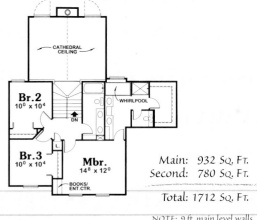

CATHEDRAL CEILING
Br. 2 10⁰ x 10⁴
WHIRLPOOL
Br. 3 10⁰ x 10⁴
Mbr. 14⁸ x 12⁰
BOOKS/ ENT. CTR.

Main: 932 Sq. Ft.
Second: 780 Sq. Ft.

Total: 1712 Sq. Ft.

NOTE: 9 ft. main level walls

IMPRESSIONS— *Homes designed for the way you live*

Deming

#48B-2545   Price Code A17

This corner hutch is a great accent in the dining room.

An efficient kitchen allows guests to circulate between the two eating areas.

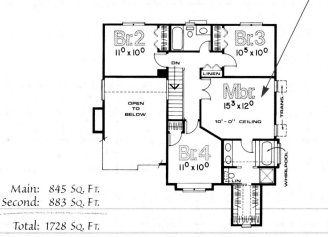

The master suite is nicely attributed with double doors, tall windows with transoms and a walk-in closet with window.

Main: 845 Sq. Ft.
Second: 883 Sq. Ft.

Total: 1728 Sq. Ft.

© design basics inc.

Mayfield

#48B-24003   Price Code A17

This large eating bar in the kitchen has room enough for the whole family to enjoy a casual meal.

A row of windows beneath an 11-foot vaulted ceiling frames a view that will be remembered in the family room.

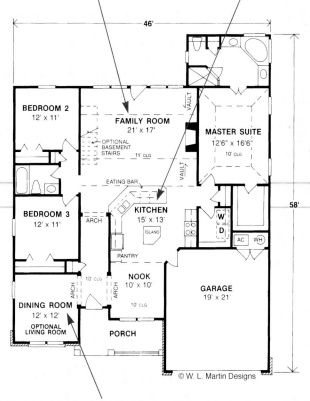

Whatever the formal needs of the homeowner, the flexibility of the dining room allows it to easily be used as a living room.

1762 Finished Sq. Ft.

Slab, Crawl Space and Basement Foundation Plans Included.

© W. L. Martin Designs

design basics inc.
HOME PLAN DESIGN SERVICE

DESIGN OPTION #13

A. THE GIFFORD
B. THE WAVERLY
C. THE TAHOE

THINK ABOUT...
FLEX SPACES

When it comes to building a home, often our budgets won't allow us to include all the elements we may need for the foreseeable future. As a result, it may merely require a bit more planning in the design of the home. Designing rooms that can be used as flex spaces is one of the easiest ways to gain more livability out of a home's floor plan. For instance, if you need both a nursery and a home office but only have the budget for one room, consider positioning that room close to the master suite and likewise in a position that would best suit your needs as home office. The room can be used for one purpose now and be adapted at a later date.

3 PERSPECTIVES...

A. The Gifford is the perfect example of a home designed for efficiency. Because of its limited square footage, bedroom 2 was designed to also function as a den.

B. The Waverly is designed to grow with the changing needs of a family. Two bedrooms are provided for the children in seclusion of the master suite. When the empty-nest situation arises, both secondary bedrooms can be altered as additional living spaces.

C. If needs change in the Tahoe, bedroom 2 can be altered to include a den. With double doors off the entry, it would make an ideal home office.

A. Gifford

#48B-2553   *Price Code* A14

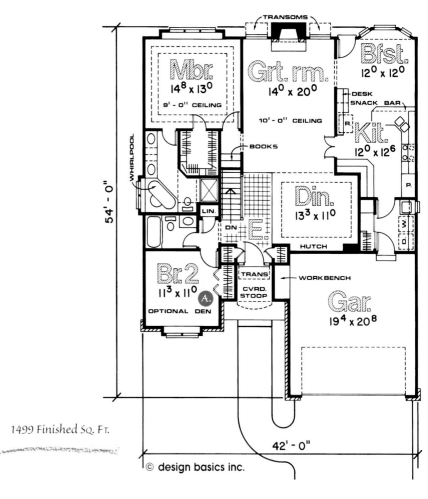

1499 Finished Sq. Ft.

© design basics inc.

B. Waverly

#48B-2355   *Price Code* A17

1710 Finished Sq. Ft.

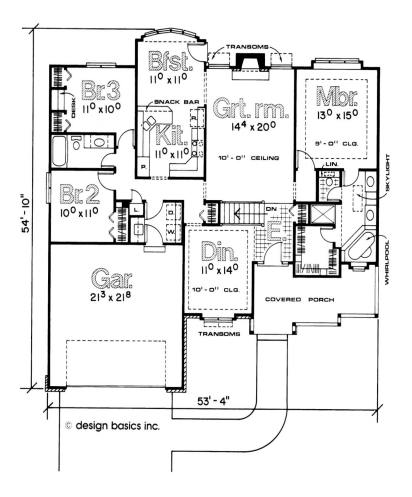

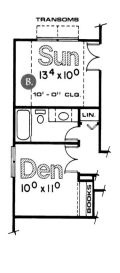

TRANSOMS

Sun
13⁴ x 10⁰
10'-0" CLG.

B.

LIN.

Den
10⁰ x 11⁰

BOOKS

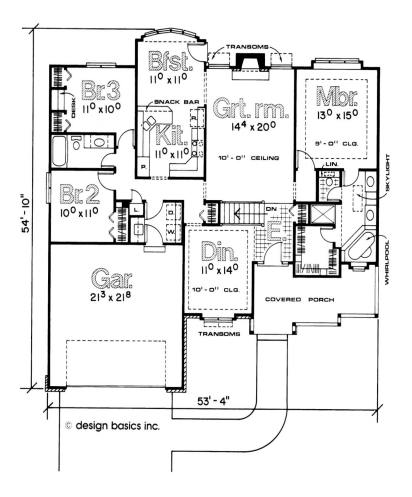

TRANSOMS

Bfst.
11⁰ x 11⁰

Br.3
11⁰ x 10⁰

DESK

SNACK BAR

Kit.
11⁰ x 11⁰

Grt. rm.
14⁴ x 20⁰

10'-0" CEILING

Mbr.
13⁰ x 15⁰

9'-0" CLG.

LIN.

SKYLIGHT

Br.2
10⁰ x 11⁰

L.

DN

WHIRLPOOL

Din.
11⁰ x 14⁰

10'-0" CLG.

Gar.
21³ x 21⁸

COVERED PORCH

54'-10"

TRANSOMS

© design basics inc.

53'-4"

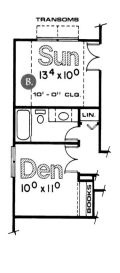

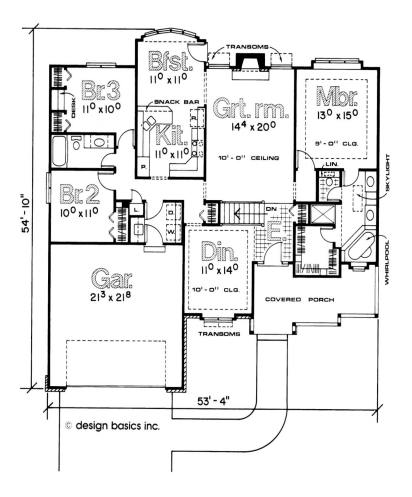

C. Tahoe

#48B-2537   *Price Code* A15

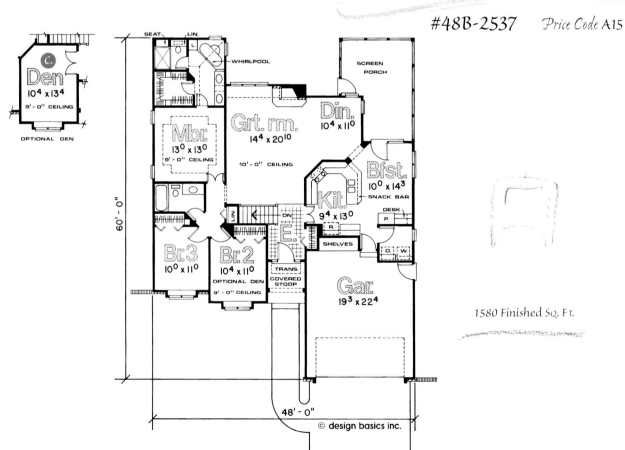

Den
10⁴ x 13⁴
9'-0" CEILING

OPTIONAL DEN

SEAT   LIN.

WHIRLPOOL

SCREEN PORCH

Mbr.
13⁰ x 13⁰
9'-0" CEILING

Grt. rm.
14⁴ x 20¹⁰
10'-0" CEILING

Din.
10⁴ x 11⁰

Bfst.
10⁰ x 14³

SNACK BAR

Kit.
9⁴ x 13⁰

DESK

P.

SHELVES

D. W.

LIN.

DN

Br. 3
10⁰ x 11⁰

Br. 2
10⁴ x 11⁰
OPTIONAL DEN
9'-0" CEILING

TRANS.
COVERED STOOP

Gar.
19³ x 22⁴

60'-0"

48'-0"

© design basics inc.

1580 Finished Sq. Ft.

54

#48B-2411   *Price Code* A36

BUILT BY: Whit Smith Construction

Le Grand

BUILT BY: Curt Hofer Construction

#48B-2218   *Price Code* A36

The breakfast area is offered beauty through bay windows with ledges.

© design basics inc.

Three fireplaces lend an overall comfortable atmosphere to this home.

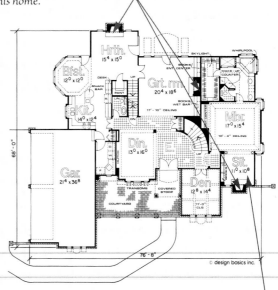

© design basics inc.

This sitting room was designed to remind those in the master suite to take refuge in relaxation.

The den is made dramatic with an arched window that pours in natural light.

Each upper-level room is a private suite and features memorable ceiling details.

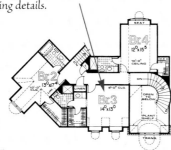

Main: 2617 Sq. Ft.
Second: 1072 Sq. Ft.

Total: 3689 Sq. Ft.

Slab and Basement Foundation Plans Included.

Main: 2603 Sq. Ft.
Second: 1020 Sq. Ft.

Total: 3623 Sq. Ft.

Slab and Basement Foundation Plans Included.

Built-in desks in the upper-level bedrooms provide a place for children to study and do homework.

HOME PLAN DESIGN SERVICE

DESIGN OPTION #14

A. THE COMSTOCK
B. THE MEREDITH
C. THE DOUGLAS

THINK ABOUT...
INFORMAL LIVING AREAS

The simplest ways in which we enjoy our homes are through our casual, day-to-day living there: reading, cooking, watching television or catching up with our kids' lives. These seemingly insignificant happenings will have great impact on the design of the informal areas of the floor plan you select. Think about whether you want informal areas to be open to each other for greater interaction or enclosed for secluded activities such as reading or phone conversations. The amenities should offer convenience, such as built-in shelves for electronic equipment– or enjoyment, such as views or a fireplace.

3 PERSPECTIVES...

A. The Comstock includes a large gathering room and kitchen with views to the back and onto a rear porch. This area is designed to include a casual arrangement of living and informal dining furniture. A built-in entertainment center and desk add to its list of everyday functionality.

B. A sunken family room in the Meredith is also privately located, but is provided interesting amenities, including a sloped ceiling, fireplace and view from an upper-level loft.

C. Placed to the rear of the Douglas, the informal family room and breakfast area both offer views to the back. This seclusion also allows children to interact at the same time formal entertaining occurs at the front of the home.

A. Comstock

#48B-2778   *Price Code* A24

2456 Finished Sq. Ft.

Slab and Basement Foundation Plans Included.

B. *Meredith*

#48B-2312   *Price Code* A21

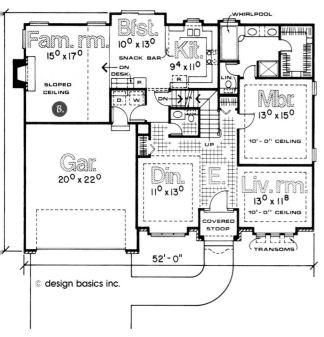

Fam. rm. 15⁰ x 17⁰
SLOPED CEILING
B.
Gar. 20⁰ x 22⁰

Bfst. 10⁰ x 13⁰
Kit. 9⁴ x 11⁰
SNACK BAR
WHIRLPOOL
DN
DESK
P.
D. W.
DN
LIN.
R.
UP

Mbr. 13⁰ x 15⁰
10'-0" CEILING

Din. 11⁰ x 13⁰
E.
Liv. rm. 13⁰ x 11⁸
10'-0" CEILING
COVERED STOOP
TRANSOMS

52'-0"

© design basics inc.

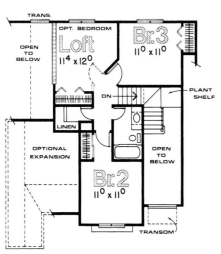

TRANS.
OPT. BEDROOM
Loft 11⁴ x 12⁰
Br. 3 11⁰ x 11⁰
OPEN TO BELOW
DN
PLANT SHELF
LINEN
OPTIONAL EXPANSION
OPEN TO BELOW
Br. 2 11⁰ x 11⁰
TRANSOM

Main: 1519 Sq. Ft.
Second: 594 Sq. Ft.

Total: 2113 Sq. Ft.

C. *Douglas*

#48B-3020   *Price Code* A22

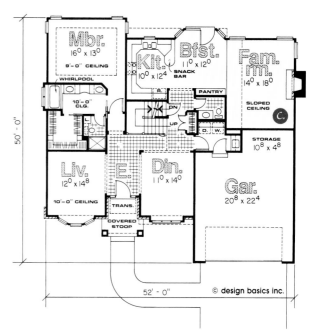

Mbr. 16⁰ x 13⁰
9'-0" CEILING
WHIRLPOOL
10'-0" CLG.

Kit. 10⁰ x 12⁴
Bfst. 11⁰ x 12⁰
SNACK BAR
R.
DN
D. W.
UP
PANTRY

Fam. rm. 14⁰ x 18⁰
SLOPED CEILING
C.
STORAGE 10⁸ x 4⁸

Liv. 12⁰ x 14⁸
10'-0" CEILING
E.
Din. 11⁰ x 14⁰
TRANS.
COVERED STOOP
Gar. 20⁸ x 22⁴

50'-0"

52'-0"   © design basics inc.

Main: 1651 Sq. Ft.
Second: 634 Sq. Ft.

Total: 2285 Sq. Ft.

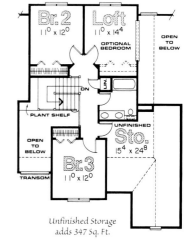

Br. 2 11⁰ x 12⁰
Loft 11⁰ x 14⁴
OPTIONAL BEDROOM
OPEN TO BELOW
DN
LIN.
PLANT SHELF
OPEN TO BELOW
Br. 3 11⁰ x 12⁰
TRANSOM
Sto. 15⁴ x 24⁸
UNFINISHED

Unfinished Storage adds 347 Sq. Ft.

HOME PLAN DESIGN SERVICE

HOME OWNER IMPRESSIONS
ON LIVING IN THE SAYLER

Of course Gus, Jaraine and their daughter Sommer were excited to move into their new home. They had spent the previous 24 years in a small, one-story home and the past 3 ½ months living with a friend until their new home, Design Basics "Sayler," was completed. They were more than ready to move in. But no one in the family was more ready or perhaps more excited, than their small West Island Terrier, Honey.

Their previous one-story home had few windows, offering much less in the way of views to the front or back. For Honey, being able to view a schoolyard from their small bedroom window was an important part of her day, though it was the only view she had for many years. By moving into the Sayler with views in most every room - Honey, you could say, was in heaven.

"When we moved in, she spent about an hour and a half inspecting the home, going from window to window in each room. I don't think she knew what to do with that many windows in the home," Jaraine said.

Honey's excitement confirmed what her owners had been trying to accomplish all along with their new home - a lot of natural light.

Another requirement for Gus and Jaraine was that the design they chose meet their needs far into the future, since they believe this will be the only home they will ever build. As a result, the master suite and laundry room locations on the main level were an important feature for them.

The master suite is Jaraine's favorite area of the

continued on page 60

58

THINK ABOUT...
STORAGE SPACE

Whether it be for seasonal items or things we just don't know where else to place, storage will always be an essential aspect of a home's design. Since most of us will only need to access storage areas a couple of times a year, it isn't essential to have ideal access to storage. One of the most practical areas for storage within a home is above the garage. This space offers a large area that doesn't take away space from the other living areas of the home. If you have special needs for storage space, make sure that it is a basic part of the home plan you select to build.

3 PERSPECTIVES...

A. A nice feature about the storage space in the Sayler is its window, which brings light into the area. This design also offers additional storage space in the garage for items such as bikes or a riding lawn mower.

B. The Wilks Manor also provides plenty of storage space in an upper-level future expansion space. This area can be finished off as the home is built, or added on later if needs demand additional storage space. Extra storage is also provided in a walk-in pantry in the kitchen.

C. Although the Oakfield is economical in size, an unfinished area above the garage provides plenty of room for storage of seasonal items. A staircase located at the rear of the garage makes this storage area easily accessible.

A. Sayler

#48B-3076   *Price Code A17*

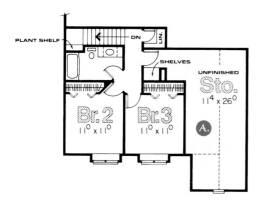

Main: 1348 Sq. Ft.
Second: 450 Sq. Ft.

Total: 1798 Sq. Ft.

Unfinished Storage adds 363 Sq. Ft.

home. She enjoys the openness provided by the 10-foot ceiling, and the amenities in the adjoining master bath. Jaraine utilizes the whirlpool tub daily and appreciates its separation from the shower so that she and Gus can get ready simultaneously.

Gus describes the Sayler as a "user-friendly" home. The family room is his favorite area of the home with its natural lighting, openness and its 10-foot ceiling. Gus and Jaraine also included a three-season porch off the back of the family room, which has also become a favorite area for the family to relax.

They also took advantage of the storage areas the Sayler provided. They utilized the extra space in the garage to include a powder bath and extend the laundry room. And the storage area on the upper level was finished into a living area for, Sommer, a 21-year-old college student.

"I think the thing I like about this home the most is that no matter what the occasion is, the home feels so comfortable and casual," Sommer says.

Their Terrier, Honey made it clear what she enjoys the most. Then as in now, she'll be content with the view.

B. Wilks Manor

#48B- 9165   *Price Code* B26

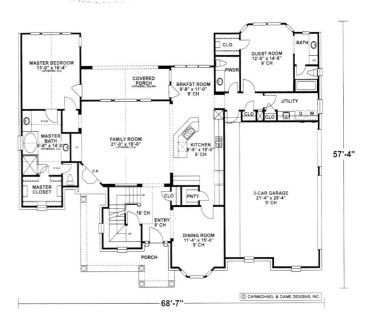

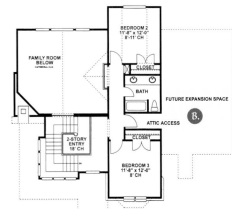

Main: 2087 Sq. Ft.
Second: 552 Sq. Ft.

Total: 2639 Sq. Ft.

Slab and Basement Foundation Plans Included.

C. Oakfield

#48B-5479   *Price Code* A11

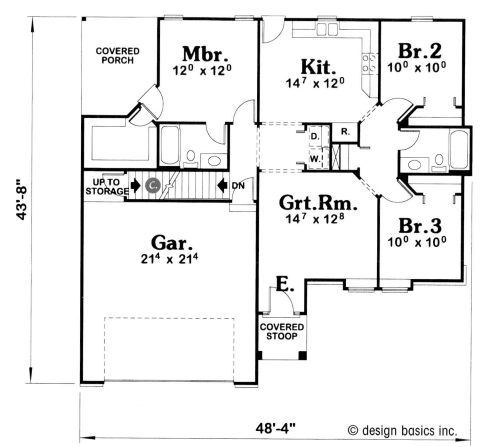

COVERED PORCH

Mbr.
12⁰ x 12⁰

Kit.
14⁷ x 12⁰

Br. 2
10⁰ x 10⁰

D.

R.

W.I.

UP TO STORAGE   C.   DN

Gar.
21⁴ x 21⁴

Grt. Rm.
14⁷ x 12⁸

Br. 3
10⁰ x 10⁰

E.

COVERED STOOP

43'-8"

48'-4"

© design basics inc.

1191 Finished Sq. Ft.

NOTE: 9 ft. main level walls

ORDER DIRECT — (800) 947-7526   www.designbasics.com

Austin

#48B-2305   *Price Code* A18

#48B-8024   *Price Code* A22

In this plan, the kitchen is the cornerstone between the open formal and informal areas.

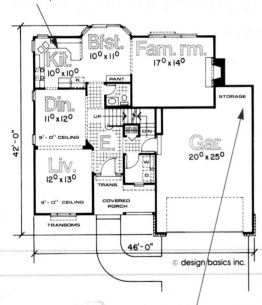

Bay windows and a fireplace will accompany casual conversation in the family room.

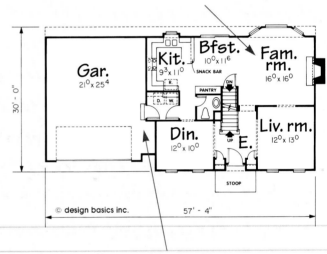

This garage alcove is ideal for including storage shelves.

Shelves or a workbench will fit neatly into this storage area in the garage.

His-and-her vanities and a massive walk-in closet offer convenience in the master suite.

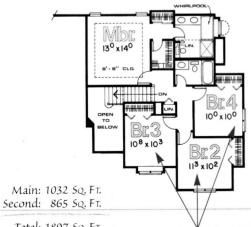

Main: 1032 Sq. Ft.
Second: 865 Sq. Ft.

Total: 1897 Sq. Ft.

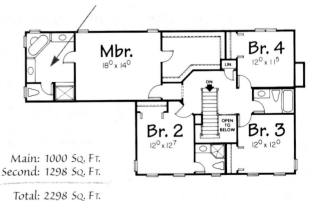

Main: 1000 Sq. Ft.
Second: 1298 Sq. Ft.

Total: 2298 Sq. Ft.

Three additional bedrooms are positioned in a cluster to allow a bit more privacy for the master suite.

A. Wrenwood

#48B-3005 *Price Code A21*

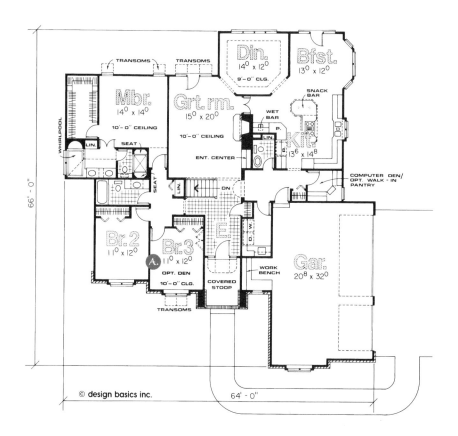

2186 Finished Sq. Ft.

THINK ABOUT...
COMPUTER SPACE

Having a place to put the family computer is almost as important these days as a place to keep the toaster. Selecting a place for the computer in your home should encompass the needs of its users. If you prefer to supervise your children as they use the computer, you may want to consider an open location. If paperwork tends to pile up near your computer, you may prefer a secluded location. Computer space needn't be large, it just needs to be accessible to everyone in the home and not crowd into rooms meant for everyday living, such as the kitchen or great room.

3 PERSPECTIVES...

A. The computer den in the Wrenwood doesn't take up a lot of extra living space from the home. This den is out of sight from the rest of the home and provides a quiet place to work.

B. Children with homework will appreciate the loft in the Ridgeville. The loft provides some seclusion on the upper level, yet can easily be accessed by all members of the home.

C. The Stanfield offers more than one option for placement of a computer. An upper-level loft allows open supervision while using the computer. Unfinished storage space can also be utilized for a more private location.

B. Ridgeville

#48B-5502   Price Code A21

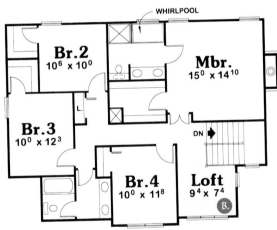

WHIRLPOOL

Br.2
10^6 x 10^0

Mbr.
15^0 x 14^{10}

L.

Br.3
10^0 x 12^3

DN

Br.4
10^0 x 11^8

Loft
9^4 x 7^4

B.

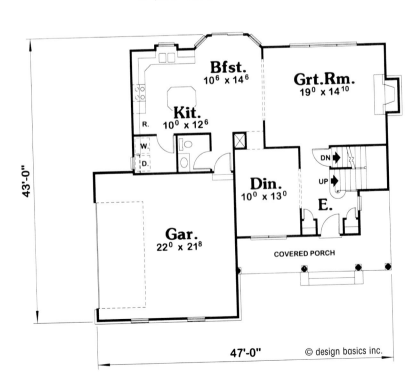

Bfst.
10^6 x 14^6

Grt.Rm.
19^0 x 14^{10}

Kit.
10^0 x 12^6

R.

W.

D.

43'-0"

DN

UP

Din.
10^0 x 13^0

E.

Gar.
22^0 x 21^8

COVERED PORCH

47'-0"   © design basics inc.

Main: 1006 Sq. Ft.
Second: 1099 Sq. Ft.

Total: 2105 Sq. Ft.

NOTE: 9 ft. main level walls

DESIGNERS'INK

IMPRESSIONS– *Homes designed for the way you live*

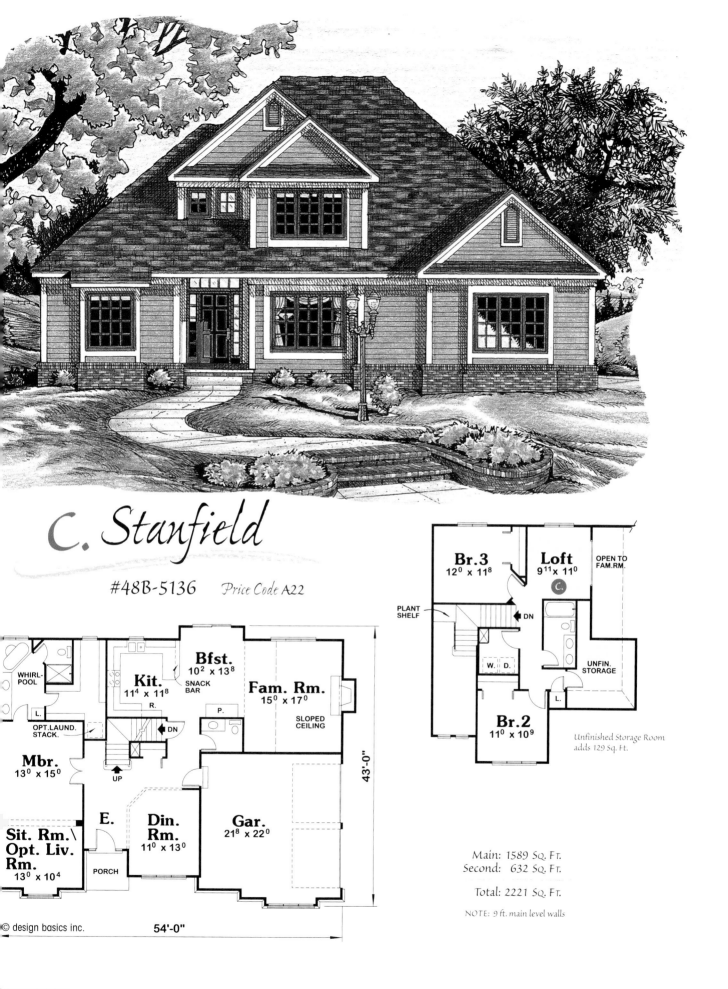

C. Stanfield

#48B-5136   *Price Code A22*

Second Floor

Br. 3
12^0 x 11^8

Loft
9^{11} x 11^0

OPEN TO FAM. RM.

PLANT SHELF

DN

W. D.

UNFIN. STORAGE

L.

Br. 2
11^0 x 10^9

Unfinished Storage Room adds 129 Sq. Ft.

Main Floor

WHIRL-POOL

L.

OPT. LAUND. STACK.

Kit.
11^4 x 11^8

SNACK BAR

R.

Bfst.
10^2 x 13^8

Fam. Rm.
15^0 x 17^0

SLOPED CEILING

P.

DN

UP

Mbr.
13^0 x 15^0

Sit. Rm.\ Opt. Liv. Rm.
13^0 x 10^4

E.

PORCH

Din. Rm.
11^0 x 13^0

Gar.
21^8 x 22^0

43'-0"

54'-0"

© design basics inc.

Main: 1589 Sq. Ft.
Second: 632 Sq. Ft.

Total: 2221 Sq. Ft.

NOTE: 9 ft. main level walls

DESIGN OPTION #17

A. THE WINGHAM COURT
B. THE PHILIPSBURG
C. THE DOVER

THINK ABOUT...
FIREPLACE LOCATION

Fireplaces, once an essential element in every home, are now merely an element we desire because of the way they make us feel and how their presence seems to change a room. Fireplaces are meant to be enjoyed, so think about the areas where you spend most of your time. Likewise, consider the size of the home you are to build and what kind of fireplace is appropriate. Would you enjoy a fireplace in your master suite or den? Is your lifestyle such that a gas vent fireplace would best suit you? Or do your prefer a natural wood fireplace?

3 PERSPECTIVES...

A. The formal and informal living areas of the Wingham Court enjoy a see-through fireplace set at an angle. The fireplace adds drama to the living room and follows on the angle of the dining room.

B. The see-through fireplace in the Philipsburg was designed to be visible from the great room, kitchen, hearth room and breakfast area. It was particularly meant to be enjoyed in the hearth room, with nearby entertainment center and built-in bookshelves.

C. An extravagant fireplace isn't practical in the efficient Dover. However, by placing it prominently to the rear of the great room, it serves as a focal point and is also visible from the entry and kitchen.

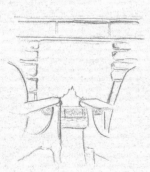

A. Wingham Court

#48B-9115   Price Code B36

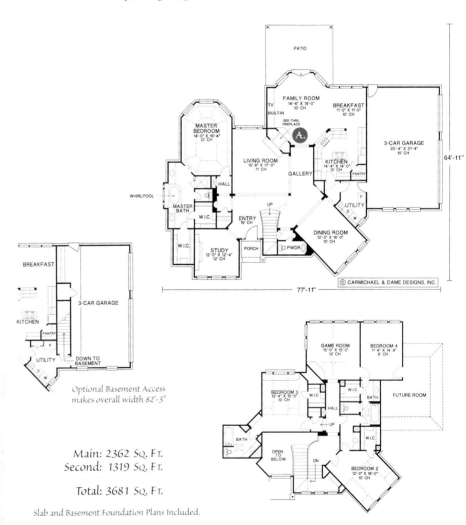

Optional Basement Access
makes overall width 82'-3"

Main: 2362 SQ. FT.
Second: 1319 SQ. FT.

Total: 3681 SQ. FT.

Slab and Basement Foundation Plans Included.

B. *Philipsburg*

#48B-5520   *Price Code* A26

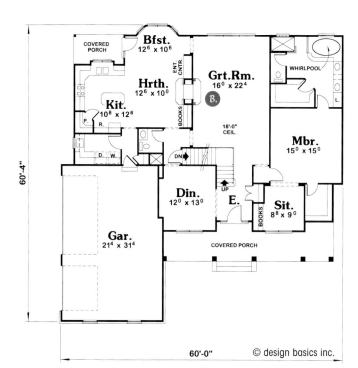

COVERED PORCH

Bfst.
$12^6 \times 10^6$

Hrth.
$12^6 \times 10^0$

Kit.
$10^8 \times 12^6$

P. R.

ENT. CNTR.

BOOKS

B.

Grt.Rm.
$16^0 \times 22^4$

WHIRLPOOL

18'-0" CEIL.

Mbr.
$15^0 \times 15^0$

DN

UP

E.

BOOKS

Din.
$12^0 \times 13^0$

Sit.
$8^8 \times 9^0$

D. W.

Gar.
$21^4 \times 31^4$

COVERED PORCH

60'-4"

60'-0"

© design basics inc.

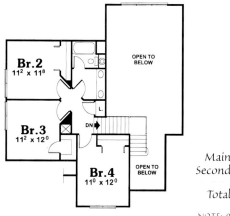

Br.2
$11^2 \times 11^8$

Br.3
$11^2 \times 12^0$

Br.4
$11^0 \times 12^0$

OPEN TO BELOW

OPEN TO BELOW

DN

L

C. *Dover*

#48B-2376   *Price Code* A12

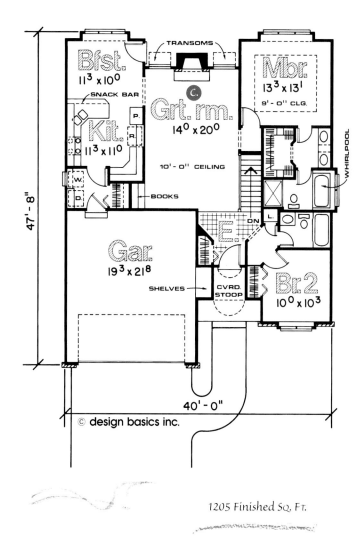

Bfst.
$11^3 \times 10^0$

SNACK BAR

TRANSOMS

C.

Mbr.
$13^3 \times 13^1$

$9'$-$0''$ CLG.

Kit.
$11^3 \times 11^0$

P. R.

Grt. rm.
$14^0 \times 20^0$

$10'$-$0''$ CEILING

WHIRLPOOL

W D

BOOKS

DN

L

Gar.
$19^3 \times 21^8$

E.

Br. 2
$10^0 \times 10^3$

SHELVES

CVRD. STOOP

47'-8"

40'-0"

© design basics inc.

Main: 1955 SQ. FT.
Second: 660 SQ. FT.

Total: 2615 SQ. FT.

NOTE: 9 ft. main level walls

1205 Finished SQ. FT.

BUILT BY: Feledy Construction

Andover

#48B-1863   Price Code A19

Main: 1421 Sq. Ft.
Second: 578 Sq. Ft.

Total: 1999 Sq. Ft.

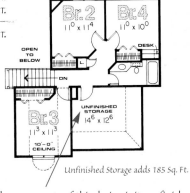

Unfinished Storage adds 185 Sq. Ft.

One of the more welcome aspects of this design is its unfinished storage area on the second floor which could be finished into a home office or retreat.

Tall windows in the great room and bayed windows in the breakfast area fill the home with plenty of natural light.

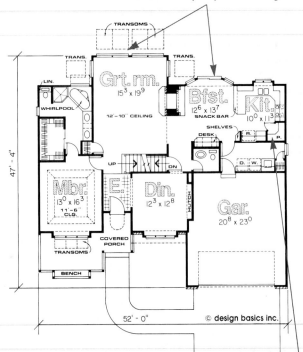

© design basics inc.

A walk-in pantry will be welcome in this organized kitchen.

Franklin

#48B-2316   Price Code A23

BUILT BY: Paradise Homes, Inc.

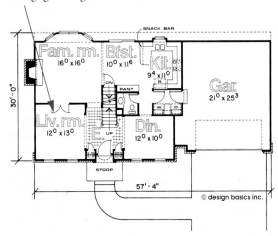

This set of French doors can expand either room for large gatherings.

© design basics inc.

Two walk-in closets, a sitting room and built-in shelves can all be found in the master suite.

Guests will appreciate bedroom 2 with its own ¾ bath.

Main: 1000 Sq. Ft.
Second: 1345 Sq. Ft.

Total: 2345 Sq. Ft.

Slab and Basement Foundation Plans Included.

IMPRESSIONS- *Homes designed for the way you live*

BUILT BY: Blake Homes

#48B-8012   *Price Code* A22

BUILT BY: Einsphar Construction

Trenton

#48B-1330   *Price Code* A18

The windows with transoms create a great deal of impact in the great room.

This see-through fireplace will create a comfortable atmosphere in the breakfast area.

A nice feature in any kitchen, and especially this one, is a walk-in pantry for storage.

OPEN TO
GREAT ROOM

Main: 1421 Sq. Ft.
Second: 448 Sq. Ft.

Total: 1869 Sq. Ft.

Slab and Basement Foundation Plans Included.

Interior views in the entry and stairway take you to the great room with fireplace and windows to the front and rear.

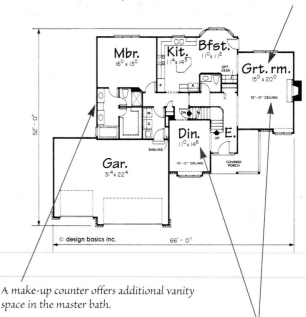

A make-up counter offers additional vanity space in the master bath.

Ten-foot ceilings avoid a congested feeling in the dining and great rooms.

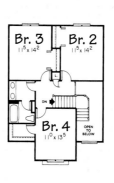

Main: 1530 Sq. Ft.
Second: 736 Sq. Ft.

Total: 2266 Sq. Ft.

Slab and Basement Foundation Plans Included.

DESIGN OPTION #18

A. THE ROBINS LANE
B. THE WINDCREST
C. THE DARIUS

THINK ABOUT...
FUTURE SPACE

It's difficult to be fully prepared for future needs. That's why you may want to consider a floor plan that offers a future use room. Typically finished over the garage or on the upper level, future space is an area large enough to be later utilized for storage or extra living space. Will you need an extra bedroom for a child? Would a playroom for the kids be just what you need? Will your job change and you'll need a home office? Including a future space in the design of your home now, can save you a worrisome dilemma in the future.

3 PERSPECTIVES...

A. Located off the master bath, the future space in the Robins Lane provides the ability to finish off a private sitting room, exercise area or even a nursery.

B. Unfinished storage space in the Windcrest is accessible off the second-level corridor. This makes the space perfect for another bedroom or other living space that can be utilized by everyone.

C. The future space in the Darius is located off the walk-in closet in the master suite. This offers the perfect opportunity to expand the master bath or incorporate a cedar closet for clothing storage.

A. Robins Lane

#48B-8031   Price Code A20

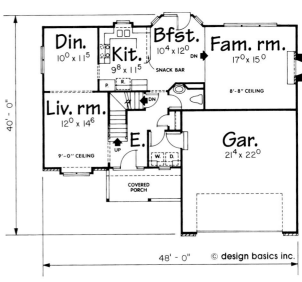

Din. 10⁰ x 11⁵
Kit. 9⁸ x 11⁵
Bfst. 10⁴ x 12⁰
Fam. rm. 17⁰ x 15⁰
SNACK BAR
8'-8" CEILING
Liv. rm. 12⁰ x 14⁶
9'-0" CEILING
E.
UP
Gar. 21⁴ x 22⁰
W. D.
COVERED PORCH
DN
40' - 0"
48' - 0"
© design basics inc.

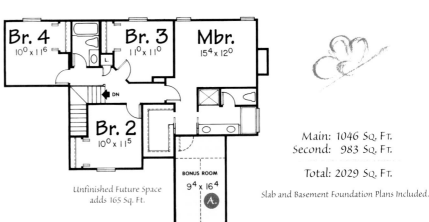

Br. 4 10⁰ x 11⁶
Br. 3 11⁰ x 11⁰
Mbr. 15⁴ x 12⁰
Br. 2 10⁰ x 11⁵
DN
BONUS ROOM 9⁴ x 16⁴
A.

Unfinished Future Space adds 165 Sq. Ft.

Main: 1046 Sq. Ft.
Second: 983 Sq. Ft.

Total: 2029 Sq. Ft.

Slab and Basement Foundation Plans Included.

IMPRESSIONS- *Homes designed for the way you live*

B. *Windcrest*

#48B-5509   *Price Code A27*

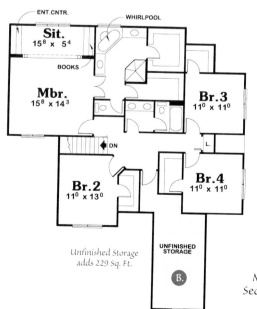

Sit.
$15^8 \times 5^4$

ENT.CNTR.   WHIRLPOOL

BOOKS

Mbr.
$15^8 \times 14^3$

Br.3
$11^0 \times 11^0$

DN

L.

Br.2
$11^0 \times 13^0$

Br.4
$11^0 \times 11^0$

Unfinished Storage adds 229 Sq. Ft.

UNFINISHED STORAGE

B.

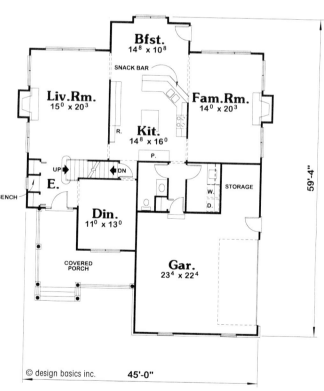

Bfst.
$14^8 \times 10^8$

SNACK BAR

Liv.Rm.
$15^0 \times 20^3$

Fam.Rm.
$14^0 \times 20^3$

R.

Kit.
$14^8 \times 16^0$

UP   DN

P.

E.

BENCH

Din.
$11^0 \times 13^0$

W.
D.

STORAGE

COVERED PORCH

Gar.
$23^4 \times 22^4$

59'-4"

© design basics inc.   45'-0"

Main: 1465 Sq. Ft.
Second: 1316 Sq. Ft.

Total: 2781 Sq. Ft.

NOTE: 9 ft. main level walls

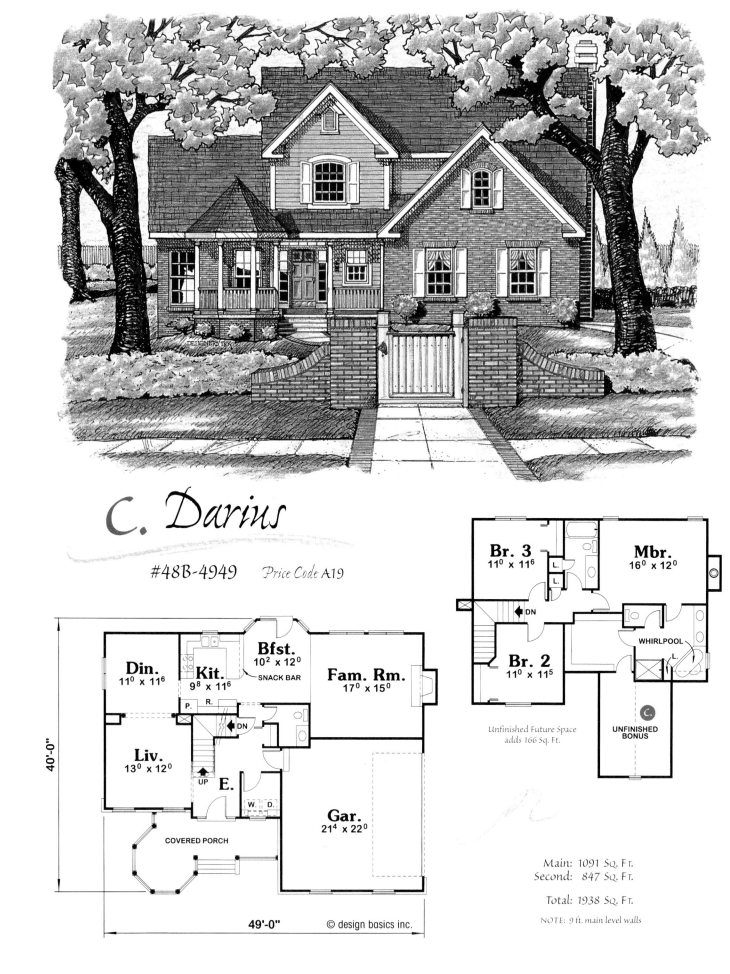

C. Darius

#48B-4949   *Price Code* A19

Br. 3
11⁰ x 11⁶

Mbr.
16⁰ x 12⁰

Br. 2
11⁰ x 11⁵

WHIRLPOOL

Unfinished Future Space adds 166 Sq. Ft.

UNFINISHED BONUS

Din.
11⁰ x 11⁶

Kit.
9⁸ x 11⁶

Bfst.
10² x 12⁰
SNACK BAR

Fam. Rm.
17⁰ x 15⁰

Liv.
13⁰ x 12⁰

DN

R.

P.

UP

E.

W.   D.

Gar.
21⁴ x 22⁰

COVERED PORCH

40'-0"

49'-0"

© design basics inc.

Main: 1091 Sq. Ft.
Second: 847 Sq. Ft.

Total: 1938 Sq. Ft.

NOTE: 9 ft. main level walls

IMPRESSIONS- *Homes designed for the way you live*

Jamestown

48B-3459   *Price Code* A15

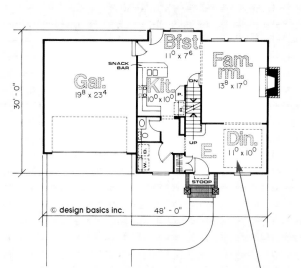

© design basics inc.   48' - 0"

This dining room welcomes guests off the entry and could easily convert into a sitting area.

Those additional bedrooms are compact and each provides a small sitting area by a window.

Main: 807 Sq. Ft.
Second: 754 Sq. Ft.

Total: 1561 Sq. Ft.

Slab and Basement Foundation Plans Included.

French doors open to his-and-her vanities and an optional whirlpool tub in the master bath.

Ohern

#48B-2569   *Price Code* A18

A 10-foot ceiling will make the kitchen and breakfast area feel more spacious when guests gather there.

This entry has a long view through the great room and out its tall windows to the rear.

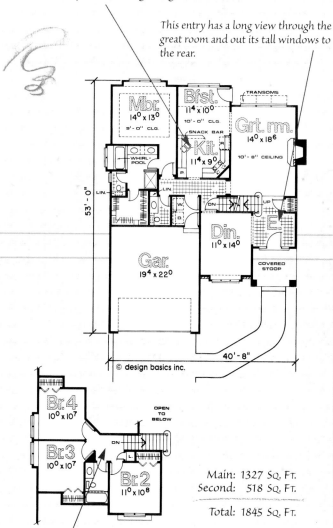

© design basics inc.   40' - 8"

Main: 1327 Sq. Ft.
Second: 518 Sq. Ft.

Total: 1845 Sq. Ft.

Though efficient in size, each upper-level room enjoys a special window.

HOME PLAN DESIGN SERVICE

HOME OWNER IMPRESSIONS

ON LIVING IN THE SAWYER

On a typical weekend morning at Mary's house you might hear the soft rattle and spray of the washing machine, the slurp of the coffee maker and maybe -

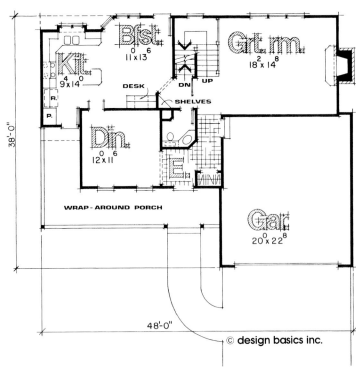

if you listen hard enough - the rustle of a newspaper. And if the phone doesn't ring, Mary may not even talk at all this day. She'll take care of her bills in the master suite. And she'll sit out on her front porch or back deck. Some may call this quiet activity, serenity. Mary calls it home - on the weekends at least. During the week her life is filled with the busy, day-to-day management of a cable company. In pace with corporate America, her job has required that she often relocate. In the past several years, she has averaged about a year and a half at any given location, she says. In fact, the four years she's currently been at her east coast location has almost taken her aback.

"I'm actually starting to think about painting the walls in my home a different color," she says with a chuckle.

Her needs in looking for a new home were quite different from the families who have had the luxury of seeing a labor of love come to fruition before their very eyes. When she moved into the area, Mary needed a new home, and she needed it right away.

Among the homes she looked at was Design Basics' "Sawyer," a new home built on speculation by a local builder.

"The outward appearance of the home grabbed my attention right away," she says. "On the inside, the thing that struck me was the spaciousness of the kitchen."

Mary says she doesn't entertain as much as she'd like, but when she does the kitchen becomes the focal point. The kitchen's finish work - all white cabinetry and tiled

continued on page 76

THINK ABOUT...
LAUNDRY ROOM LOCATION

While we'd rather not have to include it, the laundry room is, nevertheless, a necessary part of the design of any home. When pondering the laundry room in your home, consider convenience first. For some, that means locating the laundry room near the bedrooms, where most of the laundry is generated. For others, a location near the kitchen where they often work is a better design. Don't forget to think about the amenities in your laundry room. A soaking sink, window and space for an ironing board are all things to consider when planning this area. After all, the easier it is for you to complete the laundry, the more time you'll have to enjoy the more enjoyable places within your new home.

3 PERSPECTIVES...

A. The two-story Sawyer features its laundry room on the second level. This location is not only convenient to all the bedrooms, it also allows square footage on the main level to be more efficiently utilized.

B. Both a soaking sink and window are great options in the Meadow Creek's laundry room. Located near the kitchen, it cuts down on noise in the living and sleeping areas.

C. In the Spring Valley, the laundry room is positioned near the bedrooms. It is out of sight of the living areas of the home and makes it easy for children to help out with the laundry.

A. Sawyer

#48B-1179   Price Code A20

Main: 927 SQ. FT.
Second: 1163 SQ. FT.

Total: 2090 SQ. FT.

flooring - helped create the pristine atmosphere that helped her eventually decide to purchase the home.

Of course the kitchen alone didn't cinch the sale. The Sawyer features a wide variety of additional attributes from which Mary continues to benefit.

Convenience was major consideration in the purchase of a home for Mary. The laundry room location on the second level of the home, was a key benefit, she says. She also spends a lot of time in the master suite, to which the builder added a sitting room.

"I think this home is a lot more livable than other places I've lived," she says. "It's not a typical design where the staircase is right in the entry. The staircase is set back somewhat, which makes both second and main levels of the home really accessible."

She also says the home's overall design helps to cut down on sound travel from room to room.

One of the most notable assets of the Sawyer is its wrap-around front porch with access from both the front door and the kitchen. Consequently, it is also a place where you can often find Mary when she's home.

"Previously I lived in Colorado and loved the atmosphere of the mountains and nature. The front porch and rear deck really lend themselves to enjoying that kind of atmosphere. The front porch, with its two access points, is really like having another living area out there," she says.

All of the home's attributes help Mary to recharge at the end of many long days and weeks.

"It's my own little nest where I can go to recoup," she says. And save a phone call or two, there's little chance she'll be disturbed.

B. Meadow Creek

#48B- 8077   *Price Code* A18

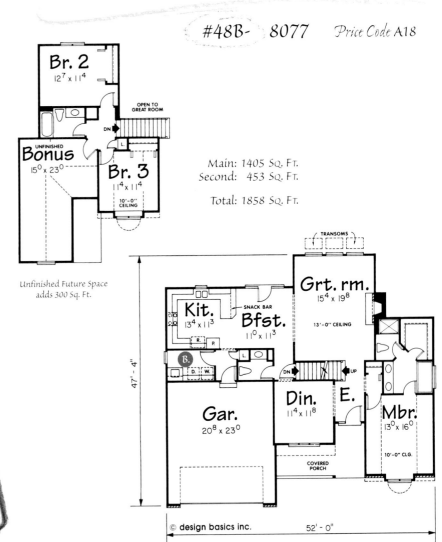

Br. 2
12⁷ x 11⁴

OPEN TO GREAT ROOM

DN

Bonus
UNFINISHED
15⁰ x 23⁰

Br. 3
11⁴ x 11⁴
10'-0" CEILING

Unfinished Future Space
adds 300 Sq. Ft.

Main: 1405 Sq. Ft.
Second: 453 Sq. Ft.

Total: 1858 Sq. Ft.

TRANSOMS

Kit.
13⁴ x 11³
SNACK BAR

Bfst.
11⁰ x 11³

Grt. rm.
15⁴ x 19⁸
13'-0" CEILING

47' - 4"

Gar.
20⁸ x 23⁰

Din.
11⁴ x 11⁸

E.

Mbr.
13⁰ x 16⁰
10'-0" CLG.

DN   UP

COVERED PORCH

© design basics inc.   52' - 0"

IMPRESSIONS- *Homes designed for the way you liv*

C. Spring Valley

#48B-8090   *Price Code* A14

Mbr.
14⁰ x 12⁰

OPTIONAL BEDROOM

1453 Finished Sq. Ft.

TRANS.   TRANS.

Bfst.
12⁰ x 10⁰

Grt. rm.
15⁰ x 18⁰
10'-0" CEILING

Mbr.
14⁰ x 14⁴

Kit.
12⁰ x 11⁴

PANT.

Gar.
21⁴ x 21⁸

E.

Br. 3
10⁰ x 10⁰

Br. 2
10⁰ x 11²

W. D.

C.

DN

R.

44' - 0"

COVERED PORCH

© design basics inc.   48' - 8"

 HOME PLAN DESIGN SERVICE

ORDER DIRECT- (800) 947-7526   www.designbasics.com   **77**

Logan

#48B-1551 *Price Code* A12

Cohasset

#48B-5084 *Price Code* A18

These built-in shelves in the family room make sense for those who want space for electronic equipment or family photos.

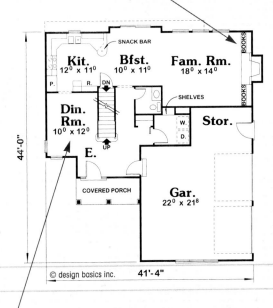

SNACK BAR

Kit.
12⁰ x 11⁰

Bfst.
10⁰ x 11⁰

Fam. Rm.
18⁰ x 14⁰

BOOKS

P.

R.

DN

SHELVES

BOOKS

Din. Rm.
10⁰ x 12⁰

W.

D.

Stor.

E.

UP

44'-0"

COVERED PORCH

Gar.
22⁰ x 21⁸

© design basics inc.

41'-4"

The open dining room has a natural appeal. And it can easily be used as a second living area, if desired.

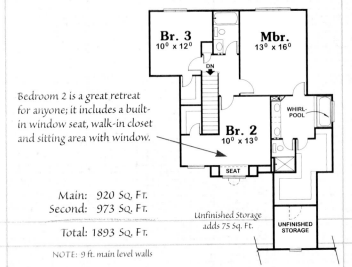

Br. 3
10⁰ x 12⁰

Mbr.
13⁰ x 16⁰

DN

WHIRL-POOL

Br. 2
10⁰ x 13⁰

SEAT

Bedroom 2 is a great retreat for anyone; it includes a built-in window seat, walk-in closet and sitting area with window.

Main: 920 SQ. FT.
Second: 973 SQ. FT.

Total: 1893 SQ. FT.

Unfinished Storage adds 75 SQ. FT.

UNFINISHED STORAGE

NOTE: 9 ft. main level walls

When eating meals, you can enjoy a view out two sides of windows in the dinette.

This laundry closet is positioned near the bedrooms for efficiency.

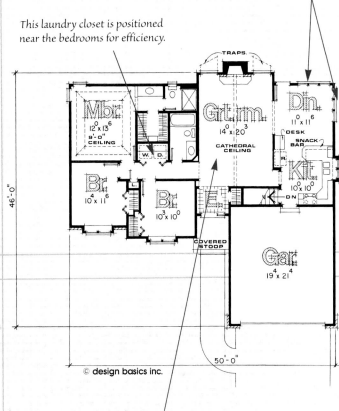

TRAPS.

Mbr.
12 x 13⁶
9'-0" CEILING

Gr. rm.
14⁰ x 20³
CATHEDRAL CEILING

Din.
11⁰ x 11⁰

DESK

SNACK BAR

Kit.
10⁰ x 10⁰

Br.
10⁴ x 11⁶

W. D.

Br.
10³ x 10⁰

E.

DN

46'-0"

COVERED STOOP

Gar
19⁴ x 21⁴

© design basics inc.

50'-0"

The great room has a dramatic feel with a cathedral ceiling that centers on a fireplace and trapezoid windows.

1271 Finished SQ. FT.

Slab and Basement Foundation Plans Included.

IMPRESSIONS- *Homes designed for the way you liv*

A. THE ORCHARD
B. THE DRAKEWOOD MANOR
C. THE HILLSBORO

THINK ABOUT...
GARAGE DESIGN

When considering your garage, note that its position will almost exclusively be determined by the type and considerations of your lot. Some covenants require a sideload position or rear-entry position for your garage. Therefore, it's important to know your lot restrictions before selecting the desired position of your garage. However, if you have your heart set on a certain location or design for your garage, you may want to take that into consideration before you select your lot.

3 PERSPECTIVES...

A. The Orchard reveals the way a three-car garage can be minimized on the front elevation. The third stall of this garage is recessed and could be easily be altered to include a tandem drive-through.

B. If you desire a sideload garage, but you're lot won't allow it, consider the garage design of the Drakewood Manor. It accomplishes a sideload garage, with an entry to the inside.

C. Out of sight of the front of the home, the three-car garage of the Hillsboro is located to the back of the home. It features double doors that would allow a golf cart direct access outdoors.

A. Orchard

#48B-2818   Price Code A16

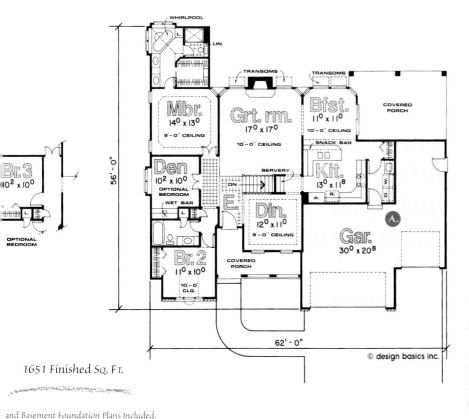

1651 Finished Sq. Ft.

and Basement Foundation Plans Included.

B. Drakewood Manor

#48B-9138 *Price Code* B33

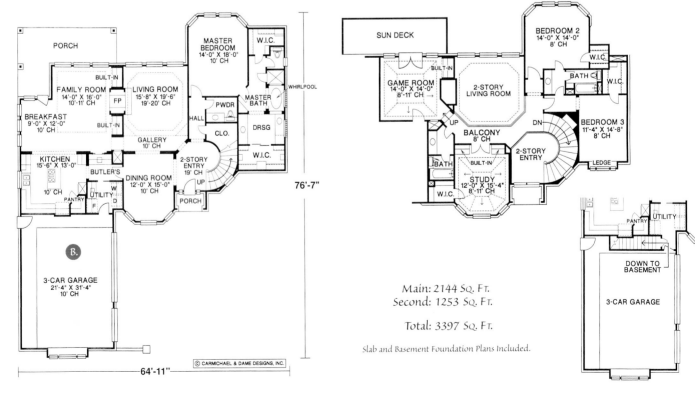

Main: 2144 SQ. FT.
Second: 1253 SQ. FT.

Total: 3397 SQ. FT.

Slab and Basement Foundation Plans Included.

© CARMICHAEL & DAME DESIGNS, INC.

64'-11"

76'-7"

Main floor labels:
PORCH
BUILT-IN
FAMILY ROOM 14'-0" X 16'-0" 10'-11" CH
BREAKFAST 9'-0" X 12'-0" 10' CH
BUILT-IN
KITCHEN 15'-6" X 13'-0" 10' CH
BUTLER'S
PANTRY
UTILITY
W D
F
LIVING ROOM 15'-8" X 19'-6" 19'-20' CH
FP
GALLERY 10' CH
DINING ROOM 12'-0" X 15'-0" 10' CH
2-STORY ENTRY 19' CH
UP
PORCH
HALL
PWDR
CLO.
MASTER BEDROOM 14'-0" X 18'-0" 10' CH
W.I.C.
MASTER BATH
DRSG
W.I.C.
WHIRLPOOL
3-CAR GARAGE 21'-4" X 31'-4" 10' CH
B.

Second floor labels:
SUN DECK
BUILT-IN
GAME ROOM 14'-0" X 14'-0" 8'-11" CH
2-STORY LIVING ROOM
UP
BALCONY 8' CH
BATH
BUILT-IN
STUDY 12'-0" X 15'-4" 8'-11" CH
W.I.C.
2-STORY ENTRY
DN
BEDROOM 2 14'-0" X 14'-0" 8' CH
W.I.C.
BATH
W.I.C.
BEDROOM 3 11'-4" X 14'-8" 8' CH
LEDGE
PANTRY
UTILITY
DOWN TO BASEMENT
3-CAR GARAGE

IMPRESSIONS– *Homes designed for the way you liv*

C. Hillsboro

#48B-2472   *Price Code A24*

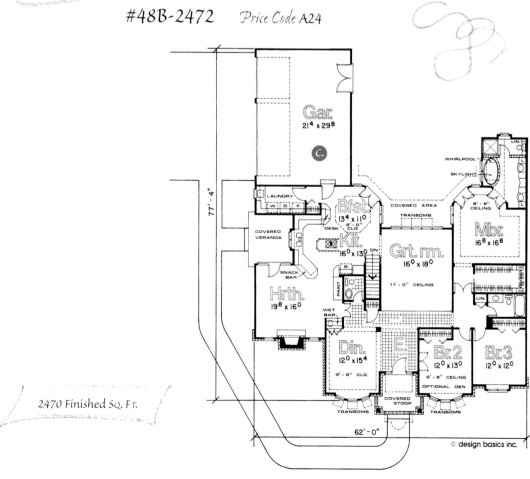

2470 Finished Sq. Ft.

Gar.
21⁴ x 29⁸

LAUNDRY
W D F

COVERED VERANDA

Bfst.
13⁴ x 11⁰
DESK   9'-0" CLG.

Kit.
16⁰ x 13⁰

SNACK BAR

Hrth.
19⁸ x 16⁰

WET BAR

PANT.

Din.
12⁰ x 15⁴
9'-8" CLG.

COVERED AREA
TRANSOMS

Grt. rm.
16⁰ x 18⁰
11'-0" CEILING

DN

WHIRLPOOL
SKYLIGHT

LIN.

Mbr.
16⁸ x 16⁸

9'-8" CEILING

LIN.

E.

Br.2
12⁰ x 13⁰
9'-8" CEILING
OPTIONAL DEN

Br.3
12⁰ x 12⁰

COVERED STOOP
TRANSOMS   TRANSOMS

77'-4"

62'-0"

© design basics inc.

THINK ABOUT
WHAT YOU WANT IN YOUR NEW HOME

For each of the following sections, first describe your current home, then compare your answers with what you are looking for in a new home. Be sure to note what you like best about your current home and consider your daily lifestyle – hobbies, recreational activities, formal and informal entertaining, etc.

HOMESITE PREFERENCES

Desired areas / subdivisions / neighborhoods _____

If new construction, have you already purchased the lot? _____

If yes, list specifics regarding lot: _____ **Width** _____ **Dept**

Special views _____

Other considerations _____

CURRENT HOME

TYPE
1-story _____
1 ½-story _____
2-story _____

SIZE
approx. finished square feet:
    main level _____
    2nd level _____
    bsmt./other _____

BEDROOMS / BATHS
number of bedrooms _____
master bedroom location _____
master suite amenities _____
closet space (lineal feet of hanging) _____
number of lavs in bath _____
whirlpool tub _____
skylight(s) _____
other _____
number of secondary bathroom locations _____

GARAGE
orientation _____
number of stalls _____

NEW HOME

TYPE
1-story _____
1 ½-story _____
2-story _____

SIZE
approx. finished square feet:
    main level _____
    2nd level _____
    bsmt./other _____

BEDROOMS / BATHS
number of bedrooms _____
master bedroom location _____
master suite amenities _____
closet space (lineal feet of hanging) _____
number of lavs in bath _____
whirlpool tub _____
skylight(s) _____
other _____
number of secondary bathroom locations _____

GARAGE
orientation _____
number of stalls _____

CURRENT HOME

FORMAL LIVING SPACES

DINING ROOM
approximate size _____

hutch or any special furniture considerations _____

_____

other considerations _____

LIVING ROOM
approx. size _____

special furniture considerations _____

specific amenities (i.e., fireplace or high ceilings) _____

_____

SEMI-FORMAL LIVING SPACE

GREAT ROOM
approximate size _____

special furniture considerations _____

specific amenities _____

INFORMAL LIVING SPACE

FAMILY ROOM
approximate size _____

special furniture considerations _____

specific amenities _____

DEN/LIBRARY/HOME OFFICE
approximate size _____

HEARTH ROOM
(a casual area for groups of 2-4 people offering a fireplace and other cozy amenities) _____

KITCHEN
eating area (dinette) within or adjacent? _____

island _____

snack bar/counter _____

planning desk_____

other amenities _____

LAUNDRY
location (main floor/2nd floor/bsmt.) _____

other considerations _____

MISCELLANEOUS
front porch/veranda _____

rear deck/covered patio _____

finished basement and uses _____

other _____

NEW HOME

FORMAL LIVING SPACES

DINING ROOM
approximate size _____

hutch or any special furniture considerations _____

_____

other considerations _____

LIVING ROOM
approx. size _____

special furniture considerations _____

specific amenities (i.e., fireplace or high ceilings) _____

_____

SEMI-FORMAL LIVING SPACE

GREAT ROOM
approximate size _____

special furniture considerations _____

specific amenities _____

INFORMAL LIVING SPACE

FAMILY ROOM
approximate size _____

special furniture considerations _____

specific amenities _____

DEN/LIBRARY/HOME OFFICE
approximate size _____

HEARTH ROOM
(a casual area for groups of 2-4 people offering a fireplace and other cozy amenities) _____

KITCHEN
eating area (dinette) within or adjacent? _____

island _____

snack bar/counter _____

planning desk_____

other amenities _____

LAUNDRY
location (main floor/2nd floor/bsmt.) _____

other considerations _____

MISCELLANEOUS
front porch/veranda _____

rear deck/covered patio _____

finished basement and uses _____

other _____

CUSTOMIZED PLAN CHANGES

PRICE SCHEDULE

ALL PLANS *Customizable*

2 X 6 EXTERIOR WALLS FROM STANDARD 2 X 4 TO 2 X 6 EXTERIOR WALLS	$175 .....
EACH GARAGE ALTERATION • FRONT-ENTRY TO SIDE LOAD (OR VICE VERSA) • 2-CAR TO 3-CAR (OR VICE VERSA) • 2-CAR FRONT-ENTRY TO 3-CAR SIDE -LOAD (OR VICE VERSA) • 3-CAR FRONT-ENTRY TO 2-CAR SIDE -LOAD (OR VICE VERSA)	$325 .....
WALK-OUT BASEMENT	$195 .....
CRAWL SPACE FOUNDATION	$250 .....
SLAB FOUNDATION	$250 .....
STRETCH CHANGES	$6 per lineal foot of cut
ADDITIONAL BRICK TO SIDES & REAR	$350 .....
ADDITIONAL BRICK TO FRONT, SIDES AND REAR	$450 .....
ALTERNATE PRELIMINARY ELEVATION	$195 .....
9-FOOT MAIN LEVEL WALLS	starting at $195
SPECIFY WINDOW BRAND (WITHOUT OTHER CHANGES - $150)	$95 .....
POURED CONCRETE FOUNDATION ONLY WITH OTHER CHANGES (WITHOUT OTHER CHANGES - $150)	$25 .....
ADDING ONE COURSE (8") TO THE FOUNDATION HEIGHT ONLY WITH OTHER CHANGES (WITHOUT OTHER CHANGES - $150)	$25 .....

NOTE

- All plan changes come to you on erasable, reproducible vellums.
- An unchanged set of original vellums is available for only $50 along with your plan changes.
- Design Basics changes are not made to the artist's renderings, electrical, sections or cabinets.
- Prices are subject to change.

As a part of our commitment to help you achieve the "perfect" home, we offer an extensive variety of plan changes for any Design Basics plan. For those whose decision to purchase a home plan is contingent upon the feasibility of a plan change, our Customer Support Specialists will, in most cases, be able to provide a FREE price quote for the changes.

call us toll-free at

(800) 947-7526

to order plan changes listed here, or if you have questions regarding plan changes not listed.

COPYRIGHT
Cans & Cannots

These days it seems almost everybody has a question about what can or cannot be done with copywritten home plans. At Design Basics, we know U.S. copyright law can sometimes get complex and confusing, but here are a few of the basic points of the law you'll want to remember.

Once you've purchased a plan from us and have received a Design Basics construction license.

PROTECT YOUR RIGHTS
to build, modify and reproduce our home plans with a Design Basics construction license.

You Can ...

■ Construct the plan as originally designed, or change it to meet your specific needs.
■ Build it as many times as you wish *without* additional re-use fees.
■ Make duplicate blueprint copies as needed for construction.

You Cannot ...

■ Build our plans without a Design Basics construction license.
■ Copy *any* part of our original designs to create another design of your own.
■ Claim copyright on changes you make to our plans.
■ Give a plan to someone else for construction purposes.
■ Sell the plan.

The above points are provided as general guidelines only. Additional information is provided with each home plan purchase, or is available upon request at (800) 947-7526.

Space Planning PRODUCTS & SERVICES

Great Ways to Simplify Your Life

For many home buyers, visualizing the finished home is a challenge. Our **Study Print & Furniture Layout Guide**™ makes it easy. First, the Study Print provides views of all exterior elevations. Secondly, the Furniture Layout Guide provides a "Feel" for room sizes, with a 1/4" scale floor plan, over 100 reusable furniture pieces and helpful tips on space planning.

– Available for any Design Basics plan –

only $29.95

STUDY PRINT & FURNITURE LAYOUT GUIDE

48B

CUSTOM FURNITURE PLANS™

❖ **Our interior designers use practical design guidelines to ensure each room has proper circulation, clearances and activity space.**

❖ **Our designers will also offer recommendations, such as custom changes or new furniture, that will make your design more functional for you.**

❖ **A unique benefit we offer is that you do not have to purchase a plan before utilizing our service. As a result, you will receive peace of mind from knowing that the design you select will meet your needs.**

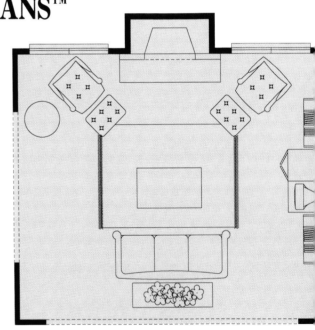

Custom Furniture Plan™ (not to scale)

48B

only $39.95
per room

DESIGN BASICS' HOME PLAN LIBRARY

1.

2.

3.

4.

5.

6.

7. 8. 9.

10. 11. 12. 13. 14. 15.

1) Easy Living One-Story Designs™ – *155 one-story home designs from the Gold Seal™, Heartland Home Plans™ and Timeless Legacy™ collections, together in one plan book.* $7.95

2) Timeless Legacy™, A Collection of Fine Home Designs by Carmichael & Dame – *52 breathtaking luxury home designs from 3300' to 4500'. Includes artful rear views of each home.* $25.00

3) Photographed Portraits of an American Home™ – *100 of our finest designs, beautifully photographed and tastefully presented among charming photo album memories of "home". A must for any sales center's coffee table.* $14.95

4) Reflections of an American Home™ Vol. III – *50 photographed home plans with warm remembrances of home and beautiful interior presentations. From 1341' to 3775'.* $4.95

5) The Narrow Home Plan™ Collection – *258 one-story, 1 ½ story and 2-story home plans that are from 26 to 50 feet wide. Many can be joined together to create customized duplex plans.* $14.95

6) Heartland Home Plans™ – *120 plan ideas designed for everyday practicality. Warm, unpretentious elevations easily adapt to individual lifestyles. From 1212' to 2631'.* $8.95

7) Nostalgia Home Plans Collection™ – A New Approach to Time-Honored Design – *70 designs showcasing enchanting details and unique "special places." From 1339' to 3480'.* $9.95

8) Nostalgia Home Plans Collection™ Vol. II - A New Approach to Time-Honored Design – *70 designs bringing back the essence of homes of the past.* $9.95

9) Gold Seal™ Home Plan Book Set – *442 of today's most sought-after one-story, 1 ½ story and 2-story home plan ideas.*

All 5 books for $84.95 or $19.95 each

- Homes of Distinction – 86 plans under 1800'
- Homes of Sophistication – 106 plans, 1800'-2199'
- Homes of Elegance – 107 plans, 2200'-2599'
- Homes of Prominence – 75 plans, 2600'-2999'
- Homes of Grandeur – 68 plans, 3000'-4000'

10) Gold Seal Favorites™ – *100 best selling plans from the famous Gold Seal™ Collection, including 25 duplex designs.* $6.95

11) *Seasons of Life™ – Designs for Reaping the Rewards of Autumn – *100 home plans specially tailored to today's empty-nester. From 1212' to 3904'.* $4.95

12) *Seasons of Life™ – Designs for Living Summer's Journey – *100 designs for the move-up buyer. From 1605' to 3775'.* $4.95

13) *Seasons of Life™ – Designs for Spring's New Beginnings – *100 home plans for first-time buyers. Presentations unique to this lifestyle. From 1125' to 2537'.* $4.95

14) Impressions of Home™ – Homes designed with the look you want – *100 designs from 1339' to 4139'.* $4.95

15) Impressions of Home™ – Homes designed for the way you live – *100 designs from 1191' to 4228'.* $4.95

*Order the complete Seasons of Life™ set (all three books) for only $9.00

48B

A Plan From Design Basics: What's In It For You?

Plans come to you on high-quality reproducible vellums and include the following:

1. Cover Page. Each Design Basics home plan features the rendered elevation and informative reference sections including: general notes and design criteria;* abbreviations; and symbols for your Design Basics' plan.

2. Elevations. Drafted at 1/4" scale for the front and 1/8" scale for the rear and sides. All elevations are detailed and an aerial view of the roof is provided, showing all hips, valleys and ridges.

3. Foundations. Drafted at 1/4" scale. Block foundations and basements are standard. We also show the HVAC equipment, structural information,* steel beam and pole locations and the direction and spacing of the floor system above.

4. Main Level Floor Plan. 1/4" scale. Fully dimensioned from stud to stud for ease of framing. 2"x4" walls are standard. The detailed drawings include such things as structural header locations, framing layout and kitchen layout.

5. Second Level Floor Plan. 1/4" scale. Dimensioned from stud to stud and drafted to the same degree of detail as the main level floor plan.*

6. Interior Elevations. Useful for the cabinet and bidding process, this page shows all kitchen and bathroom cabinets as well as any other cabinet elevations.

7. Electrical and Sections. Illustrated on a separate page for clarity, the electrical plan shows suggested electrical layout for the foundation, main and second level floor plans. Typical wall, cantilever, stair, brick and fireplace sections are provided to further explain construction of these areas.

All plan orders received prior to 2:00 p.m. CT will be processed, inspected and shipped out the same afternoon via 2nc ness day air within the continental United All other product orders will be sent vi ground service. Full Technical Support is av for any plan purchase from Design Basic. Technical Support Specialists provide unli technical support free of charge and answer que regarding construction methods, framing technique more. Please call 800-947-7526 for more information.

CONSTRUCTION LICENSE

When you purchase a Design Basics home plan, you rece Construction License which gives you certain rights in building the depicted in that plan, including:

No Re-Use Fee. As the original purchaser of a Design Basics home plan, the Const License permits you to build the plan as many times as you like.

Local Modifications. The Construction License allows you to make modifications t Design Basics plans. We offer a complete custom change service, or you may ha desired changes done locally by a qualified draftsman, designer, architect or engineer.

Running Blueprints. Your plans are sent to you on vellum paper that reproduces v your blueprint machine. The Construction License authorizes you or your blueprint at your direction, to make as many copies of the plan from the vellum masters as you for construction purposes.

* Our plans are drafted to meet average conditions and codes in the state of Nebraska, at the time they are designed. Because codes and requirements can change and may vary from jurisdiction to jurisdiction, Design Basics Inc. cannot warrant compliance with any specific regulation. All Design Basics plans can be adapted to your local building codes and requirements. It is the responsibility of the purchaser and/or builder of each plan to see that the structure is built in strict compliance with all governing municipal codes (city, county, state and fe

✔	HOME PLAN PRODUCTS	PLAN #	QTY.	PRICE	SHIPPING & HANDLING	TOTAL
☐	1 Complete Set of Master Reproducible/Modifiable Vellum Prints					$
☐	Add'l. Sets of Blueprints - $20.00 Plan #9115-#9119-#9138-#9157-#9159-#9165-#9166 – $40.00					$
☐	Add'l. Sets of Mirror Reverse Blueprints - $20.00 Plan #9115-#9119-#9138-#9157-#9159-#9165-#9166 – $40.00					$
☐	Materials & Estimator's Workbook - $50.00 (Not Available for plans #9119-#9157-#24003-#24006-#24007)					$
☐	Study Print & Furniture Layout Guide - $29.95 *Study print only for #9115-#9119-#9138-#9157-#9159 – $25					$
☐	Custom Furniture Plans™ - $39.95 (Not Available for plans #9115-#9119-#9138-#9157-#9159-#9165-#9166-#24003-#24006-#24007)					$
☐	Plan Book Deal – $100.00					$

BOOK NUMBER	BOOK NAME			
				$
				$

• CALL FOR •
Shipping & Handling Charges

PLAN PRICE SCHEDULE
FOR ONE SET OF MASTER VELLUMS

Plan Price Code	Total Sq. Ft.	A	B
11	1100' - 1199'	$495	—
12	1200' - 1299'	$505	—
13	1300' - 1399'	$515	—
14	1400' - 1499'	$525	—
15	1500' - 1599'	$535	—
16	1600' - 1699'	$545	—
17	1700' - 1799'	$555	—
18	1800' - 1899'	$565	—
19	1900' - 1999'	$575	—
20	2000' - 2099'	$585	—
21	2100' - 2199'	$595	—
22	2200' - 2299'	$605	—
23	2300' - 2399'	$615	$6
24	2400' - 2499'	$625	$6
25	2500' - 2599'	$635	—
26	2600' - 2699'	$645	$6
27	2700' - 2799'	$655	—
28	2800' - 2899'	$665	—
29	2900' - 2999'	$675	—
30	3000' - 3099'	$685	—
31	3100' - 3199'	$695	—
32	3200' - 3299'	$705	—
33	3300' - 3399'	$715	$7
34	3400' - 3499'	$725	$7
35	3500' - 3599'	—	$7
36	3600' - 3699'	$745	$7
37	3700' - 3799'	$755	—
38	3800' - 3899'	$765	—
42	3900' - 3999'		$8

• No COD Orders • US Funds Only •
NO REFUNDS OR EXCHANGES, PLEASE

CALL 800-947-7526
ASK FOR DEPT. 48B
OR MAIL ORDER TO: **Design Basics**
11112 John Galt Blvd.
Omaha, NE 68137

Subtotal	$	
TX Res. Add 6.25% Tax (on #9115-#9119-#9138-#9157-#9159-#9165 &#9166 only) NE Residents Add 6.5% Sales Tax	$	
Total	$	

PRICES SUBJECT TO CHANGE